That Manuscript from Outer Space

That Manuscript From Outer Space

H. L. Willmington

THOMAS NELSON INC., PUBLISHERS
Nashville New York

Third printing

Second updated edition, published by Old-Time Gospel Hour, 1987

Published in Nashville, Tennessee, by Thomas Nelson Inc., Publishers, and simultaneously in Don Mills, Ontario, by Thomas Nelson & Sons (Canada) Limited. Manufactured in the United States of America.

Unless otherwise indicated, all Bible verses are taken from the King James Version.

Verses marked TLB are taken from *The Living Bible* (Wheaton, Illinois: Tyndale House Publishers, 1971) and are used by permission.

Verses marked NASB are from the *New American Standard Bible*, © The Lockman Foundation 1960, 1962, 1963, 1968, 1971, 1972, 1973, 1975, and are used by permission.

Credit: Portions of *None of These Diseases* by S. I. McMillan, Copyright © 1963 by Fleming H. Revell Company, used by permission.

Library of Congress Cataloging in Publication Data

Willmington, H L
That manuscript from outer space.

Includes bibliographical references.
1. Bible—Evidences, authority, etc. 2. Bible—Criticism, interpretation, etc. I. Title.
BS480.W525 1977 220.6 77-23596
ISBN 0-8407-9503-3

Contents

This book is dedicated
to my beloved students,
those faithful men and women
enrolled in the Thomas Road Bible Institute.
I have found their daily desire
is that expressed by King David
who once prayed:

> "Open thou mine eyes, that I may behold
> wondrous things out of thy Law."
> (Ps. 119:18)

H. L. Willmington
Dean, Thomas Road Bible Institute
Lynchburg, Virginia

Foreword

Dr. Harold Willmington has been a close friend of mine for several years. I preached in both the large and small churches he has pastored. I personally consider him one of the best Bible teachers in America. I felt that way for a long time. When I was executive vice president at Lynchburg Baptist College, Dr. Jerry Falwell asked that I find the best man to be dean of Thomas Road Bible Institute. There was no one else in my thinking. I invited Willmington to give special Bible lectures at Lynchburg Baptist College. Immediately the students loved his Bible teaching, but he wanted to stay in the pastorate. When he returned for a second Bible lectureship, the thrill of teaching captured his soul and he became dean of the Bible Institute. The testimonies of those who have gone through his classes only reinforce my previous opinion of his teaching ability.

Willmington has a rare combination of scholarship and heart appeal. I once characterized him as making a refreshing return to the original Bible institute hermeneutics that blend grammatical interpretation with an appealing presentation. I personally believe the great Bible institutes of the twenties and thirties were killed by rational Christianity. They were built on Bible knowledge that convinced the mind and fed the heart, but somewhere teachers forgot the Bible came from life and must be applied back to life. I feel the example of Harold Willmington and the Thomas Road Bible Institute can help restore the Great Bible institutes of the past.

Those who study this book on the Bible will capture the spirit that has made Harold Willmington successful. He believes every word in the Bible is inspired of God, not only to be a perfect doctrinal statement, but "The Word of God is quick (living) and powerful and sharper than a two-edged sword" (Heb. 4:12). The Bible is in-breathed with God's spirit so that those who read and believe will be filled with the life of God—eternal life (2 Pet. 1:4). After all is said and done, this is why the true teacher instructs the Bible.

May God bless this volume with the degree of influence it deserves. May He bless it because it magnifies His Word.

Elmer L. Towns
Savannah, Ga.

PART ONE
How the Bible Came Into Being

Everybody knows the Bible has been and continues to be the world's best seller, but not everybody knows just how this amazing Book came down to us today. It *could* have happened this way: At some early ecumenical "scripture session," a group of prophets and priests got together in Jerusalem to write a religious best seller. A committee was soon formed which assigned the books, appointed the authors, and arranged for all other details. Upon completion, the publicity chairman commissioned the Palestinian Press to print up the first one million copies. We said it *could* have happened that way. But of course it didn't! God used three wonderful methods as He carefully carved out that most blessed of all books, the Bible! These three "tools of the Trinity" are referred to as *revelation, inspiration* and *illumination*. Let us use an earthly story to illustrate this.

Over fifty years ago a famous German scientist named Albert Einstein developed a very important mathematical concept of the nature of our universe. Let us suppose that during this time he suddenly summons you into his home for a secret conference. He invites you to be seated and immediately explains why you have been asked to come. He begins: "I have just completed one of the most comprehensive scientific theories since the days of Sir Isaac Newton. I want you to write this all down on paper and send it to the news media of the world. Here is my astonishing theory—energy equals the mass times the speed of light squared ($E=mc_2$)!"

He then goes on to explain how mass and energy are equivalent, and that the property called mass is simply concentrated energy. You are awed as he continues with his amazing grasp of the universe. Finally he stops and says: "Now I want you to write this all down in your own words, but in order to make sure you get everything right, I want to help you in choosing those words."

So the next few hours are spent in this manner. Dr. Einstein gently but firmly guides you in the selection of the verbs and nouns from your own vocabulary. At long last you have it all down, the exact and complete revelation of truth from Albert Einstein described perfectly in your own handwriting and from your personal reservoir of words.

Before you leave, the aged scientist speaks once again: "One final thing that will encourage you: I plan to call every important newspaper and television editor, telling them the message they will receive from you is true and they should both believe it and publish it!"

Here we have an example (however weak) of God's three tools and how they function. *Revelation* occurred when Dr. Einstein called you in and imparted to you his great truth. *Inspiration* took place when he guided you as you wrote it down. *Illumination* happened when he encouraged the news editor to accept his report as given by you.

How then did we receive our Bible? Well, around 1400 B.C. God began to quietly call some forty men and women into His presence. Oh, He didn't call them in all at once, mind you. In fact, it took Him nearly fifteen centuries to complete the job. He spoke the burden of His great heart in simple but sublime language to those chosen forty. With a holy hush they heard Him tell of creation and corruption, of condemnation, of justification, sanctification, and glorification! Weighty words, indeed! When he had finished, the first tool in carving out the Bible was set aside. *Revelation* had occurred!

Now we see this almighty Author as He quickly but carefully guides each chosen human vessel in his assigned writing task. Each of the forty is dealt with individually. Job, a rich farmer, will write differently than will Amos, a poor farmer. The words of the educated Paul will be more complicated on occasion than those of the uneducated John or Peter. But all will carry with them the divine approval of heaven itself.

Finally, the last scribe lays down his (or her) pen. The angels watch as their Creator lays aside the second tool in the making of His manuscript. *Inspiration* has taken place.

Soon many thousands of men and women join the ranks of those original forty and begin their assigned task of taking God's glory story to the uttermost parts of the earth. As they do, untold multitudes are stopped in their tracks, convinced in their hearts, and saved from their sins! By what secret power did all this take place? The answer is simple: the Author of the Bible is using the third and final tool. *Illumination* continues to take place.

And so the Scriptures are shaped. To summarize thus far, think of the three tools as follows:

REVELATION: From God to man (man hears that which God wants written)
INSPIRATION: From man to paper (man writes that which God wants written)
ILLUMINATION: From paper to heart (man receives that which God has written)

Now that we have observed the purpose of these three tools, let us turn our thoughts to the nature of each weapon. We have examined the fruit of the tools, but what of the root? How did God make the weapon itself? We first consider:

I. Revelation

We know God spoke to man, but how did He speak? Hebrews 1:1 informs us He spoke to the fathers and prophets in many ways. A careful examination of the Bible reveals at least eight different modes of communication. These are:

A. He often spoke to men through angels. Consider:
   1. Angels reassured Abraham of the birth of Isaac and informed him of God's decision to destroy Sodom, Genesis 18.
   2. Angels warned Lot to flee Sodom before that awful destruction took place, Genesis 19.
   3. The angel Gabriel explained the nature of the Tribulation to Daniel, Dan. 9:21-27.
   4. Gabriel informed Zacharias he would have a son who would become the forerunner of Christ, Luke 1:11-20.
   5. Gabriel informed Mary that God had chosen her as His vessel for Christ's birth, Luke 1:26-37.
   6. Angels announced the birth of Christ to the shepherds, Luke 2:8-14.
   7. An angel announced the resurrection of Christ to some women, Matt. 28:5-7.
   8. An angel directed Philip to the seeking eunuch, Acts 8:26.
   9. An angel directed Peter out of a Roman prison, Acts 12:7-10.

B. He spoke to men through a loud voice.
   1. He spoke directly to Adam, Gen. 3:9-19.

2. He spoke directly to Noah, Gen. 6:13-21.
3. He spoke directly to Abraham, Gen. 12:1-3.
4. He spoke directly to Moses, Exod. 20:1-17.
5. He spoke directly to Joshua, Josh. 1:1-9.
6. He spoke directly to Samuel, 1 Sam. 3:1-14.
7. He spoke directly to Nathan, about David, 2 Sam. 7:4-16.
8. He spoke directly to Elijah, 1 Kings 17:2-4.
9. He spoke directly to Jeremiah, Jer. 1:4-5.

C. He spoke to men through a still, small voice, 1 Kings 19:11-12; Ps. 32:8.

D. He spoke to men through nature, Ps. 19:1-3; Rom. 1:18-20; Acts 14:15-17.

E. He spoke to one man through the mouth of an ass (Num. 22:28)! This simply has to be one of the funniest moments in the Bible!

F. He spoke to men through dreams. On a number of occasions God chose this method.

1. Jacob received the confirmation of the Abrahamic Covenant in a dream, Gen. 28:12.
2. Solomon received both wisdom and a warning in a dream, 1 Kings 3:5; 9:2.
3. Joseph in the New Testament received three messages in three dreams.
   a. Assuring him of Mary's purity, Matt. 1:20.
   b. Commanding him to flee to Egypt, Matt. 2:13.
   c. Ordering him to return to Palestine, Matt. 2:19-22.
4. The wise men were warned of Herod's evil intentions in a dream, Matt. 2:12.

G. He spoke to men through visions. Unger's Bible Dictionary defines a vision as: "A supernatural presentation of certain scenery or circumstances to the mind of a person while awake." It may be noted that many great truths in the Scriptures were related to men through this unique method.

1. Jacob was instructed in a vision to go to Egypt, Gen. 46:2.
2. David was warned of judgment in a vision, 1 Chron. 21:16.
3. Isaiah saw God's holiness in a vision, Isa. 6:1-8.
4. Daniel saw the great Gentile powers in a vision, Daniel 7 and 8.

5. Daniel saw the glories of Christ in a vision, Dan. 10:5-9.
6. Daniel saw the rise and fall of Alexander the Great in a vision, Daniel 8.
7. Ezekiel saw the regathering of Israel in a vision, Ezekiel 37.
8. Ananias was ordered to minister to Saul in a vision, Acts 9:10.
9. Cornelius was instructed to send for Peter in a vision, Acts 10:3-6.
10. Peter was ordered to minister to Cornelius in a vision, Acts 10:10-16.
11. Paul was ordered to Macedonia in a vision, Acts 16:9.
12. Paul was comforted at Corinth in a vision, Acts 19:9.
13. Paul was comforted at Jerusalem in a vision, Acts 23:11.
14. Paul viewed the glories of the third heaven in a vision, 2 Cor. 12:1-4.
15. The apostle John received the Book of Revelation in a vision.

H. He spoke to men through Christophanies. A Christophany is a pre-Bethlehem appearance of Christ. Some theologians have seen a number of these appearances in the Old Testament, believing that the term "the Angel of the Lord," is actually another name of Christ. If this is true, the following examples of Christophany communication could be submitted.

1. The Angel of the Lord wrestled with Jacob, Gen. 32:24-30.
2. The Angel of the Lord redeemed Jacob from all evil, Gen. 48:16.
3. The Angel of the Lord spoke to Moses from the burning bush, Exod. 3:2.
4. The Angel of the Lord protected Israel at the Red Sea, Exod. 14:19.
5. The Angel of the Lord prepared Israel for the Promised Land, Exod. 23:20-23; Ps. 34:7; Isa. 63:9; 1 Cor. 10:1-4.
6. The Angel of the Lord commissioned Gideon, Judg. 6:11.
7. The Angel of the Lord ministered to Elijah, 1 Kings 19:7.
8. The Angel of the Lord reassured Joshua, Josh. 5:13-15.
9. The Angel of the Lord saved Jerusalem, Isa. 37:36.

10. The Angel of the Lord preserved three godly Hebrew men, Dan. 3:25.

How then did God communicate His revelation to the forty human authors? To be truthful, we simply do not know. He could have used any one or a combination of these eight modes of communication as have been described above.

II. Inspiration

Thus we have discussed various possibilities and ways God may have employed in the giving of His revelation to the human authors. Now let us consider the next major step, that of inspiration. The ears have heard the message, but how will the fingers react? What is involved in transferring the voice of God into the vocabulary of man? We shall now examine five areas along this particular line. But before we do this, let us define the word itself. The term "inspiration" is found but once in the New Testament. This occurs in 2 Tim. 3:16. Here Paul says, "All scripture is given by inspiration of God . . ." The Greek word is *theopneustos,* and literally means, "God-breathed."

A. Various theories of inspiration:

1. *The Natural Theory*—This says the Bible writers were inspired in the same sense William Shakespeare was inspired. In other words, that spark of divine inspiration that supposedly is in all men simply burned a little brighter in the hearts of the Bible writers. This theory is totally rejected by the apostle Peter (2 Pet. 1:20). "Knowing this first, that no prophecy of the scripture is of any private interpretation."

2. *The Mechanical Theory*—That God coldly and woodenly dictated the Bible to His writers as an office manager would dictate an impersonal letter to his secretary. It should be noted here that the Bible is the story of divine love, and God is anything but mechanical or cold concerning this subject! The Holy Spirit therefore never transgressed the limits of the writer's vocabulary. Thus, the educated Paul uses many of the "85¢" words, while the less educated John employs more of the "25¢" words. But both writings are equally inspired by God! (See 2 Tim. 3:16.)

Here Dr. Charles Hodge has well written:

> The Church has never held what has been stigmatized as the mechanical theory of inspiration. The sacred

> writers were not machines. Their self-consciousness was not suspended; nor were their intellectual powers superseded. Holy men spoke as they were moved by the Holy Ghost. It was men not machines; not unconscious instruments, but living, thinking, willing minds, whom the Spirit used as His organs . . . The sacred writers impressed their peculiarities on their several productions as plainly as though they were the subjects of no extraordinary influence.[1]

3. *The Content (or Concept) Theory*—That only the main thought of a paragraph or chapter is inspired. This theory is immediately refuted by many biblical passages.

> For verily I say unto you, Till heaven and earth pass, one jot or one tittle shall in no wise pass from the law, till all be fulfilled (Matt. 5:18).

> Now these be the last words of David. David the son of Jesse said, and the man who was raised up on high, the anointed of the God of Jacob, and the sweet psalmist of Israel said, "The spirit of the Lord spake by me, and His word was in my tongue" (2 Sam. 23:1-2).

4. *The Partial Theory*—That only certain parts of the Bible are inspired. This of course is the position of the liberal theologian who would cheerfully accept those portions of the Bible which deal with love and brotherhood, but quickly reject the passages dealing with sin, righteousness, and future judgment. But let it be said that heaven and hell are like up and down—you can't have one without the other! Paul refutes the partial theory in 2 Tim. 3:16.

In his textbook, *Dispensational Theology,* Dr. Charles F. Baker writes:

> A certain bishop is purported to have said that he believed the Bible to have been inspired in spots. When asked for his authority for such a statement, he quoted Hebrews 1:1, stating that this meant that God spoke at various times in varying degrees. Thus, some spots were fully inspired, others were only partially inspired, and still others were not inspired at all. The bishop was em-

barrassed when a layman asked: "How do you know that Heb. 1:1, the one scripture upon which you base your argument, is one of those fully inspired spots?" [2]

5. *The Spiritual-Rule-Only Theory*—This says the Bible may be regarded as our infallible rule of faith and practice in all matters of religious, ethical, and spiritual value, but not in other matters such as some of the historical and scientific statements found in the Word of God. This is pious nonsense! Consider the following: Here is a pastor greatly beloved by his congregation. How would this man of God feel if only his "moral" and "spiritual" statements made in the pulpit were accepted by his members? How would he react when the members would smile and take lightly any scientific or historical statements he might make? The fallacy of the spiritual-rule-only theory is that any book or man whose scientific or historical statements are open to question can certainly neither be trusted in matters of moral and spiritual pronouncements! This theory is soundly refuted by Jesus Himself in John 3:12.

> If I have told you earthly things, and ye believe not, how shall ye believe, if I tell you of heavenly things?

6. *The Plenary-Verbal Theory*—That all (plenary) the very words (verbal) of the Bible are inspired by God. This view alone is the correct theory.

> But he answered and said, It is written, Man shall not live by bread alone, but by every word that proceedeth out of the mouth of God (Matt. 4:4).

> All scripture is given by inspiration of God, and is profitable for doctrine, for reproof, for correction, for instruction in righteousness: That the man of God may be perfect, thoroughly furnished unto all good works (2 Tim. 3:16-17).

> Which things also we speak, not in the words which man's wisdom teacheth, but which the Holy Ghost teacheth; comparing spiritual things with spiritual (1 Cor. 2:13).

> For I have given unto them the words which thou gavest me; and they have received them, and have known surely

> that I came out from thee and they have believed that thou didst send me (John 17:8).
>
> It is the spirit that quickeneth; the flesh profiteth nothing: the words that I speak unto you, they are spirit, and they are life (John 6:63).

B. Scripture texts on inspiration: The Bible, of course, strongly claims its writings are from God. Compiling a few choice texts we discover:

1. That no Old Testament Scripture was thought up by the prophet himself, 2 Pet. 1:20.
2. That all Old Testament Scriptures were given by the Holy Spirit as He moved upon men, 2 Pet. 1:21.
3. That this Spirit-breathed inspiration was given in many ways, Heb. 1:1.
4. That once it was given, this inspired writing:
   a. could not be broken or shaken down, John 10:35.
   b. is exact in all details, down to the smallest stroke and letter, Matt. 5:18.
   c. would abide forever, Matt. 5:18; 1 Pet. 1:25.
5. That the Old Testament writers did not always understand the nature of everything they wrote about, 1 Pet. 1:10-12; Luke 10:23-24.
   a. They did not completely understand the details of Christ's suffering.
   b. They did understand the mysteries would be clear to a generation other than theirs.
6. That the four gospels were given by inspiration of God, Heb. 1:1; 2 Pet. 3:2.
7. That Paul believed his writings were inspired by God, 1 Cor. 2:4; 15:3; 1 Thess. 2:13; 4:15.

NOTE: Some have felt Paul claimed no inspiration when he wrote certain passages in 1 Corinthians 7. Consider the following:

a. "But I speak this by permission, and not of commandment" (v. 6).
b. "But to the rest speak I, not the Lord (v. 12).
c. "Now concerning virgins I have no commandment of the Lord; yet I give my judgment . . ." (v. 25).
d. "But she is happier if she so abide, after my judgment: and I think also that I have the Spirit of God" (v. 40).

Let us now briefly examine each of these passages:

a. The word "permission" is literally "a joint opinion," and may refer to the inspired "considered opinion" of both Paul and Sosthenes. At any rate, Paul was simply saying this opinion was not a command but rather a divine suggestion. For a comparable passage, see Rom. 12:1.
b. Verse 12 can be explained by comparing it with verse 10. There, Paul quotes a command uttered by the Lord Jesus Himself while He was upon the earth (see Matt. 19:6). But here is a group situation (one partner saved, one unsaved) to which Jesus issued no command while on earth, but now does so in heaven through Paul's inspired pen!
c. The same answer given for verse 12 also applies here in verse 25.
d. The word "think" here could also be translated "persuaded." See Matt. 22:42; 1 Cor. 8:2 where the same Greek word is used.

8. That Paul used the Holy Spirit's words to explain the Holy Spirit's facts, 1 Cor. 2:13.
9. That Paul's writings were received through a special revelation from Christ, Gal. 1:11-12.
10. That Paul's writings were to be read by all, Col. 4:6; 1 Thess. 5:27.
11. That Peter believed his writings were inspired by God, 2 Pet. 3:2.
12. That Peter believed Paul's writings were inspired, 2 Pet. 3:15-16.
13. That John believed his writings were inspired, Rev. 22: 18-19. John warned:
    a. that if anyone added to His words, God would add horrible plagues to him.
    b. that if anyone subtracted from his words, God would remove his name from the Holy City.

C. Implications of inspiration: As one carefully considers the subject of inspiration, he is led to the following nine conclusions:

1. Plenary-verbal inspiration does not teach that all parts of the Bible are equally important, but only that they are equally inspired.

For example, Judg. 3:16 is obviously not as important as John 3:16, but both these verses were inspired by God:

> But Ehud made him a dagger which had two edges, of a cubit length; and he did gird it under his raiment upon his right thigh (Judg. 3:16).

> For God so loved the world that He gave His only begotten Son, that whosoever believeth in him should not perish, but have everlasting life (John 3:16).

2. Plenary-verbal inspiration does not guarantee the inspiration of any modern or ancient translation of the Bible, but deals only with the original Hebrew and Greek languages.
3. Plenary-verbal inspiration does not allow for any false teaching, but it does on occasion record the lie of someone. For example, Satan distorts the truth and lies to Eve (Gen. 3:4). Therefore we have an accurate record of the devil's words. As one reads the Bible, he must carefully distinguish between what God records and what He sanctions. Thus, while lying, murder, adultery, and polygamy are to be found in the Word of God, they are never approved by the God of the Word!
4. Plenary-verbal inspiration does not permit any historical, scientific, or prophetical error whatsoever. While it is admitted that the Bible is not a textbook on science, it is nevertheless held that every scientific statement in the Scriptures is absolutely true.
5. Plenary-verbal inspiration does not prohibit personal research. The New Testament writer Luke begins his gospel account with the following words:

> Inasmuch as many have undertaken to compile an account of the things accomplished among us, just as those who from the beginning were eyewitnesses and servants of the Word have handed them down to us, it seemed fitting for me as well, having investigated everything carefully from the beginning, to write it out . . . (Luke 1:1-3, NASB).

6. Plenary-verbal inspiration does not deny the use of extrabiblical sources. Here several examples come to mind.
   a. On at least two occasions, Paul quotes from heathen authors, Acts 17:28; Titus 1:12.

b. Jude quotes from an ancient Hebrew book, one not included in the Bible, Jude 1:14-15.

7. Plenary-verbal inspiration does not overwhelm the personality of the human author. The Bible writers experienced no coma-like trances as do some mediums during a seance, but on the contrary, always retained their physical, mental, and emotional powers. Various passages testify to this. See Isa. 6:1-11; Daniel 12.

8. Plenary-verbal inspiration does not exclude the usage of pictorial and symbolic language. This is to say the Holy Spirit does not demand we accept every word in the Bible in a wooden and legalistic way. For example, a case could not be made that God has feathers like a bird by referring to Ps. 91:4. Here the thought is simply that the persecuted believer can flee to his heavenly Father for protection and warmth!

9. Plenary-verbal inspiration does not mean uniformity in all details given in describing the same event. Here an Old Testament and a New Testament example come to mind.

a. Old Testament example: The wicked reign of King Manasseh is vividly described for us in two separate chapters. These are 2 Kings 21:1-18 and 2 Chron. 33:1-20. In 2 Kings we read only of his sinful ways, but in 2 Chronicles we are told of his eventual prayers of forgiveness and subsequent salvation. The reason for this may be that God allowed the author of 2 Kings to describe the reign of Manasseh from an earthly standpoint (even though He inspired the pen of the author), while He guided the pen of the author of 2 Chronicles to record Manasseh's reign from a heavenly viewpoint. God alone of course knows true repentance when He sees it coming from the human heart!

b. New Testament example: There are four different accounts concerning the superscription on the cross at Calvary.

(1) Matthew says—"This is Jesus the King of the Jews" (Matt. 27:37).

(2) Mark says—"The King of the Jews" (Mark 15:26).

(3) Luke says—"This is the King of the Jews" (Luke 23:38).

(4) John says—"Jesus of Nazareth the King of the Jews" (John 19:19).

The entire title probably read, "This is Jesus of Nazareth, the King of the Jews."

10. Plenary-verbal inspiration assures us God included all the necessary things He wanted us to know, and excluded everything else, 2 Tim. 3:15-17.

D. Importance of inspiration: Of the three tools involved in the making of our Bible, inspiration is the most important. This is true because—

1. One may have inspiration without revelation. We have already seen how Luke carefully checked out certain facts concerning the life of Christ and was then led to write them on paper (Luke 1:1-4; 1 John 1:1-4).
2. One may have inspiration without illumination. Peter tells us (1 Pet. 1:11) the Old Testament prophets did not always understand everything they wrote about. But without inspiration, the Bible falls!

E. Completion of Inspiration: Is inspiration still going on today? Has God inspired the writing (or will He someday) of a 67th book of the Bible? For nearly twenty centuries now, evangelical Christians everywhere have held to the belief that when John the apostle wrote Rev. 22:21 and wiped his pen, inspiration stopped! Furthermore, it is generally believed his warning not to add to nor to subtract from his book included not only the book of Revelation, but the entire Bible! (See Rev. 22:18-19.) It is of utmost importance that this is clearly understood, else the following tragic conclusions take place. If inspiration is still going on today, then one is forced to admit:

1. That God could have inspired the weird and wicked writings of a Joseph Smith, or a Mary Baker Eddy, or a Charles Russell, or a Herbert W. Armstrong.
2. That perhaps we still do not possess all the details concerning the plan of salvation, details vital to escape hell and enter heaven.
3. That God has allowed millions of devoted and faithful Christians to believe a horrible lie for some 2000 years!

III. Illumination

We have already stated that without inspiration, no Scripture would have ever been written. We may now claim that without illumination, no sinner would have ever been saved! Illumination, then, is that method used by the Holy Spirit to shed divine light upon all seeking men as they look into the Word of God. Illumination is from the written word to the human heart. Consider:

A. The reasons for illumination—Why is this third step necessary? Why cannot sinful man simply read and heed the biblical message without divine aid?

1. It is necessary because of natural blindness: Paul writes of this—

> But the natural man receiveth not the things of the Spirit of God: for they are foolishness unto him: neither can he know them, because they are spiritually discerned (1 Cor. 2:14).

Our Lord also commented on this during His earthly ministry—

> And Simon Peter answered and said, Thou art the Christ, the Son of the living God. And Jesus answered and said unto him, Blessed art thou, Simon Bar-jona: for flesh and blood hath not revealed it unto thee, but my Father which is in heaven (Matt. 16:16-17).

2. It is necessary because of satanic blindness. Again we note the sober words of Paul:

> But if our gospel be hid, it is hid to them that are lost: In whom the god of this world hath blinded the minds of them which believe not . . . (2 Cor. 4:3-4).

3. It is necessary because of carnal blindness—Heb. 5:12-14; 1 Corinthians 3; 2 Peter 1.

B. Results of illumination.

1. Sinners are saved.

> The Lord openeth the eyes of the blind . . . (Ps. 146:8). The entrance of thy words giveth light . . . (Ps. 119:130).

2. Christians are strengthened.

> As newborn babes, desire the sincere milk of the Word, that ye may grow thereby (1 Pet. 2:2).
>
> But God hath revealed them unto us by His Spirit . . . (1 Cor. 2:10).
>
> For God, who commanded the light to shine out of darkness, hath shined in our hearts, to give the light of knowledge . . . (2 Cor. 4:6).
>
> Thy Word is a lamp unto my feet, and a light unto my path (Ps. 119:105).

C. Implications of illumination.

1. The Holy Spirit looks for a certain amount of sincerity before He illuminates any human heart. We are quick to point out sincerity is not enough to save anyone. However, it should be also noted that it is equally impossible for an insincere person to be saved. This first implication is brought out in several passages.

> But without faith it is impossible to please Him: for he that cometh to God must believe that He is, and that He is a rewarder of them that diligently seek Him (Heb. 11:6).
>
> God is a spirit: and they that worship Him must worship Him in spirit and in truth (John 4:24).

Furthermore, it should be stated here that no Christian should ever look upon illumination as automatic. That is to say, God has never promised to reveal precious and profound biblical truths to any believer who will not search the Scriptures for himself.

Note the following admonitions:

> Man shall not live by bread alone, but by every word that proceedeth out of the mouth of God (Matt. 4:4).
>
> But these are written that ye might believe that Jesus is the Christ, the Son of God . . . (John 20:31).
>
> These were more noble than those in Thessalonica, in that they received the Word with all readiness of mind, and searched the Scripture daily . . . (Acts 17:11).
>
> Study to shew thyself approved unto God, a workman that

needeth not to be ashamed, rightly dividing the Word of truth (2 Tim. 2:15).

As newborn babes, desire the sincere milk of the Word, that ye might grow thereby (1 Pet. 2:2).

2. The Holy Spirit often seeks out the aid of a believer in performing His task of illuminating the hearts of others. This is seen:

a. In the ministry of Philip to the Ethiopian eunuch.

And Philip ran hither to him, and heard him read the prophet Esaias, and said, understandest thou what thou readest? And he said, how can I, except some man should guide me. . . . . Then Philip opened his mouth, and began at the same Scripture, and preached unto him Jesus (Acts 8:30, 31, 35).

b. In the ministry of Paul, to the Jews at Thessalonica.

And Paul, as his manner was, went in unto them, and three sabbath days reasoned with them out of the Scripture (Acts 17:2).

c. In the ministry of Aquila and Priscilla to Apollos.

And he began to speak boldly in the synagogue: Whom when Aquila and Priscilla had heard, they took him unto them, and expounded unto him the way of God more perfectly (Acts 18:26).

d. In the ministry of Apollos to the Jews at Corinth.

For he mightily convinced the Jews, and that publicly, shewing by the Scriptures that Jesus was Christ (Acts 18: 28).

PART TWO

How History Has Viewed the Bible

I. The Position of Israel

In spite of her sin and sorrows, Old Testament Israel held steadfast in the belief that her thirty-nine holy books were indeed the very Word of God. Even though one of her kings would attempt to burn it (Jeremiah 36), the nation as a whole would continue to believe it. The following words of Moses beautifully summarize Israel's position concerning the Word of God:

> Hear, O Israel: The Lord our God is one Lord: And thou shalt love the Lord thy God with all thine heart, and with all thy soul, and with all thy might. And these words, which I command thee this day, shall be in thine heart: And thou shalt teach them diligently unto thy children, and shalt talk of them when thou sittest in thine house, and when thou walkest by the way, and when thou liest down, and when thou risest up. And thou shalt bind them for a sign upon thine hand, and they shall be as frontlets between thine eyes. And thou shalt write them upon the posts of thy house, and on thy gates (Deut. 6:4-9).

II. The Position of the Early Church

During the third, fourth and fifth centuries the Church held no less than 184 councils, not to deal with civil rights, ecology problems, or political ills, but to deal with any and all heresy that would dare tamper with the pure Word of God.

III. The Position of Agnosticism

In the book, *A Guide to the Religions of America,* Dr. Bertrand Russell makes the following statement:

> An agnostic regards the Bible exactly as enlightened clerics regard it. He does not think that it is divinely inspired; he thinks its early history legendary, and no more exactly true than that in Homer; he thinks its moral teaching sometimes good, but sometimes very bad. For example: Samuel ordered Saul, in a war, to kill not only every man, woman, and child of the enemy, but also all the sheep and cattle. Saul, however, let the sheep and cattle live, and for this we are told to condemn him. I have never been able to admire

Elisha for cursing the children who laughed at him, or to believe (what the Bible asserts) that a benevolent Deity would send two she-bears to kill the children.[3]

IV. The Position of Liberalism

Probably the most famous liberal of the twentieth century was the late Harry Emerson Fosdick. He has written the following words which typify the liberal attitude:

> When one moves back to the Scriptures with a mind accustomed to work in modern ways he finds himself in a strange world. . . . Knowing modern astronomy he turns to the Bible to find the sun and the moon standing still on the shadow retreating on a sundial. Knowing modern biology he hears that when Elisha had been so long dead that only his bones were left, another dead body, thrown into the cave where he was buried, touched his skeleton and sprang to life again, or that after our Lord's resurrection many of the saints long deceased arose and appeared in Jerusalem. Knowing modern physics he turns to the Bible to read that light was created three days before the sun and that an axe-head floated when Elisha threw a stick into the water. Knowing modern medicine he finds in the scripture many familiar ailments, epilepsy, deafness, dumbness, blindness, insanity, ascribed to the visitation of demons . . . We live in a new world. We have not kept the forms of thought and categories of explanation in astronomy, geology, biology, which the Bible contains. We have definitely and irrevocably gotten new ones. . . .[4]

V. The Position of the Cults

In general it may be said the major cults and sects of Christianity give lip service to the Bible; they nevertheless look upon the writings of their various founders as equal if not superior to the Scriptures.

A. Christian Scientist (Founded by Mary Baker Eddy—1821-1910)—George Channing, an international Christian Science lecturer and practitioner, writes the following:

> Each person, of any religion, can find what is satisfying to him as the spiritual meaning in the Bible. But Christian Scientists feel that Mrs. Mary Baker Eddy's Book, *Scientist and Health with Key to the Scriptures,* offers the complete spiritual meaning of

the Bible. They believe that this full meaning would not have been available to them without Mrs. Eddy's discovery.[5]

B. Jehovah's Witnesses (Founded by Charles Taze Russell; 1851-1916)—Mr. Russell calmly announces in the opening pages of his *Studies in the Scriptures* that it would be far better to leave the Bible unread but read his comments on it than to omit his writings and read the Bible!

C. Mormonism (Founded by Joseph Smith; 1805-1844)—This cult teaches that the *Book of Mormon,* first printed in 1830, must be regarded on an equal basis with the Bible.

VI. The Position of Romanism

Rome believes that the Church is the divinely appointed custodian of the Bible and has the final word on what is meant in any specific passage. It accepts the apocryphal books as a part of the inspired Scriptures. Rome's position on the Bible could be diagrammed as a triangle, with the Pope at the top, and the Bible and Church tradition at the bottom.

VII. The Position of Mysticism

Those holding this view lean heavily upon that divine "inner light" to reveal and guide them into all truth. Thus the personal experiences, feelings, etc., of an individual are looked upon as vital to discovering divine truth as the Word of God itself.

VIII. The Position of Neo-orthodoxy (Popularized by Karl Barth in his *Epistle to the Romans,* first published in 1918).

This position holds the Bible may well indeed contain the Word of God, but that, until it becomes such, it is as dead and uninspired as any other ancient or modern historical book might be. Thus the Bible is not to be viewed as objective, but subjective in nature. It is only the Word of God as it becomes the Word of God to me. Neo-orthodoxy would thus view the first eleven chapters as "religious myths." This term is defined as a "conveyer of theological truth in a historical garb, but which theological truth is not dependent upon the historicity of the garb itself for its validity."

IX. The Position of Neo-Evangelicalism

In the latter part of 1957, one of the leaders of this position wrote the following:

> The New Evangelicalism in the latest dress of orthodoxy or Neo-orthodoxy is the latest expression of theological liberalism. The New Evangelicalism differs from Fundamentalism in its willingness to handle the social problems which Fundamentalism evaded. There need be no dichotomy between the personal gospel and the social gospel. . . . The New Evangelicalism has changed its strategy from one of separation to one of infiltration . . . The evangelical believes that Christianity is intellectually defensible but the Christian cannot be obscurantist in scientific questions pertaining to the Creation, the age of man, the Universality of the flood and other moot biblical questions.[6]

X. The Position of Orthodoxy

This view holds the Bible alone is the illuminated inspired revelation of God and is therefore the sole ground of authority for believers. Orthodoxy claims the Bible is objective in nature and proclaims not a social gospel, but a sinner gospel. According to this view, whenever there is a clear contradiction between the Bible and any assumed "fact" of history or science, it is those subjects which must give way to the Bible, and not the opposite!

A. This was the view of the Old Testament writers concerning the Old Testament:

1. Moses—Exod. 4:10-12
2. Samuel—1 Sam. 8:10
3. Joshua—Josh. 23:14
4. David—2 Sam. 23:2, 3
5. Isaiah—Isa. 1:10
6. Jeremiah—Jer. 1:6-9
7. Ezekiel—Ezek. 3:10-12
8. Daniel—Dan. 10:9-12
9. Joel—Joel 1:1
10. Amos—Amos 3:1
11. Obadiah—Obad. 1:1
12. Jonah—Jonah 1:1
13. Micah—Mic. 1:1
14. Naham—Nah. 1:1
15. Habakkuk—Hab. 2:2

16. Zephaniah—Zeph. 1:1
17. Haggai—Hag. 1:1
18. Zechariah—Zech. 1:1
19. Malachi—Mal. 1:1

Here it should be kept in mind that the Old Testament refers to itself as the Word of God some 3,808 times.

B. This was the view of the New Testament writers concerning the Old Testament. The New Testament writers refer to at least 161 Old Testament events and quote from over 246 Old Testament passages. Some of these events and passages are as follows:

1. Old Testament events referred to in the New Testament—(From the 161 events, 22 of the more important ones are listed here):
   a. Creation—Gen. 1:1; Heb. 11:3.
   b. Man made in God's image—Gen. 1:26; 1 Cor. 11:7.
   c. God resting—Gen. 2:2-3; Heb. 4:4.
   d. The institution of marriage—Gen. 2:24; Matt. 19:4-6.
   e. The fall—Gen. 3:6-8; Rom. 5:12-19.
   f. The murder of Abel—Gen. 4:8; 1 John 3:12.
   g. Enoch's translation—Gen. 5:21-24; Heb. 11:5.
   h. The ark of Noah—Gen. 6:14-16; 7:1-12; Luke 17:26-27; 2 Pet. 3:6.
   i. The call of Abraham—Gen. 12:1; Heb. 11:8.
   j. The meeting of Abraham and Melchizedek—Gen. 14:18-20; Heb. 7:1-4.
   k. The destruction of Sodom—Genesis 19; Matt. 11:24; Luke 17:32.
   l. Isaac's birth—Gen. 19:26; Gal. 4:23.
   m. The offering up of Isaac—Gen. 22:10; Heb. 11:17-19.
   n. The burning bush—Exod. 3:2; Luke 20:37; Acts 7:30.
   o. The Exodus—Exodus 12–14; Acts 7:36; Heb. 11:29; 1 Cor. 10:1.
   p. The giving of manna—Exod. 16:15; John 6:31.
   q. The giving of the law—Exodus 20; Gal. 3:19.
   r. The serpent of brass—Num. 21:8-9; John 3:14.
   s. Elijah and the drought—1 Kings 17; Luke 4:25; James 5:17.
   t. The healing of Naaman—2 Kings 5:14; Luke 4:27.

u. Daniel in the lion's den—Dan. 6:22; Heb. 11:33.
v. Jonah in the belly of the fish—Jonah 1:17; Matt. 12:40; 16:4.

2. Old Testament passages referred to in the New Testament.
   a. Be ye holy, for I am holy—(Lev. 11:44; 1 Pet. 1:16).
   b. I will never leave thee nor forsake thee—(Josh. 1:5; Heb. 13:5).
   c. Be ye angry and sin not—(Ps. 4:4; Eph. 4:26).
   d. There is none righteous, no not one—(Ps. 14:1; Rom. 3:10).
   e. Whom the Lord loveth he chasteneth—(Prov. 3:12; Heb. 12:6).
   f. God shall wipe away all tears from their eyes—(Isa. 25:8; Rev. 21:4).
   g. Death is swallowed up in victory—(Hos. 13:14; 1 Cor. 15:54).
   h. I will pour out my Spirit upon all flesh—(Joel 2:28; Acts 2:17).
   i. Whomsoever shall call on the name of the Lord shall be saved—(Joel 2:32; Rom. 10:13).
   j. The earth is the Lord's and the fulness thereof—(Ps. 24:1; 1 Cor. 10:26).
   k. My son, despise not the chastening of the Lord—(Prov. 3:11; Heb. 12:5).
   l. Blessed is He that cometh in the name of the Lord—(Ps. 118:26; Matt. 21:9).
   m. Charity covereth a multitude of sins—(Prov. 10:12; 1 Pet. 4:8).
   n. How beautiful are the feet of them that preach the gospel—(Isa. 52:7; Rom. 10:15).

C. This was the view of the New Testament writers concerning the New Testament:

1. Peter's testimony—2 Pet. 3:2.
2. Paul's testimony—1 Cor. 2:4, 13; 15:3; 1 Thess. 2:13; 4:15.
3. John's testimony—Rev. 22:18-19.
4. James' testimony—James 1:21; 4:5.
5. Jude's testimony—Jude 1:3.

D. This was the view of the Lord Jesus Christ concerning the entire Bible!

1. Our Lord began His ministry by quoting from the Old Testament. Compare Matt. 4:4, 7, 10 with Deut. 8:3; 6:16, 13.
2. Our Lord ended His ministry by quoting from the Old Testament. Five of His last seven statements on the cross were lifted from the pages of the Old Testament. Compare:
   Luke 23:34 with Isa. 53:12
   Luke 23:43 with Isa. 53:10, 11
   Matt. 27:46 with Ps. 22:1
   John 19:28 with Ps. 69:21
   Luke 23:46 with Ps. 31:5

3. Our Lord preached one of His first public messages from an Old Testament text. Compare Luke 4:16-19 with Isa. 61: 1-2.
4. Our Lord informed the Pharisees they erred, "not knowing the Scriptures," Matt. 22:29.
5. Our Lord justified His own actions by referring to the Old Testament.
   a. When He ate on the Sabbath—Matt. 12:1-8.
   b. When He healed on the Sabbath—Matt. 12:10-21.
   c. When He cleansed the temple—Matt. 21:13.
   d. When He accepted the praise of the crowds at His triumphal entry—Matt. 21:16.
6. Our Lord believed in the history of the Old Testament. He referred to—
   a. Creation—Mark 10:6
   b. Noah's ark—Matt. 24:38
   c. Lot's wife—Luke 17:32
   d. Destruction of Sodom—Luke 17:29
   e. Jonah and the fish—Matt. 12:40
   f. The Queen of Sheba and Solomon—Matt. 12:42
   g. The repentence of Nineveh—Matt. 12:41
   h. Naaman the leper—Luke 4:27
   i. Elijah and the widow—Luke 4:25, 26
   j. Moses and the serpent—John 3:14
   k. The first marriage—Matt. 19:5-7
   l. The blood of Abel—Luke 11:51
   m. Abraham, Isaac, and Jacob—Matt. 22:31, 32

n. The burning bush—Luke 20:37
o. The wilderness manna—John 6:31
p. The murder of Zacharias—Matt. 23:35

7. Our Lord said the law would be fulfilled (Matt. 5:18) and the Scriptures could not be broken (John 10:35).

It has been estimated that over one-tenth of Jesus' recorded New Testament words were taken from the Old Testament. In the four gospels, 180 of the 1,800 verses which report His discourses are either Old Testament quotes or Old Testament allusions.

In concluding this section it may be said that every single Old Testament book is either directly or indirectly referred to in the New Testament (with the possible exception of the Song of Solomon)! About half the great sermons in the book of Acts are composed of verses taken from the Old Testament. Peter's twenty-three-verse sermon at Pentecost takes twelve of these verses from the Old Testament (Acts 2:14-36). Stephen's forty-eight-verse message is completely Old Testament in nature (Acts 7:2-50). Paul's first recorded sermon occurring in Acts 13:16-41 is twenty-six verses long and of these, fifteen are Old Testament.

PART THREE

What Great Personalities Have Said About the Bible

I. From United States Presidents—

A. George Washington (1st) "It is impossible to rightly govern the world without the Bible."

B. John Adams (2nd) "The Bible is the best book in the world. It contains more . . . than all the libraries I have seen."

C. Thomas Jefferson (3rd) "The Bible makes the best people in the world."

D. John Quincy Adams (6th) "It is an invaluable and inexhaustible mine of knowledge and virtue."

E. Andrew Jackson (7th) "That book, sir, is the rock on which our Republic rests."

F. Zachary Taylor (12th) "It was for the love of the truths of this great book that our fathers abandoned their native shore for the wilderness."

G. Abraham Lincoln (16th) "But for this Book we could not know right from wrong. I believe the Bible is the best gift God has ever given to man."

H. Ulysses S. Grant (18th) "The Bible is the Anchor of our liberties."

I. Rutherford B. Hayes (19th) "The best religion the world has ever known is the religion of the Bible. It builds up all that is good."

J. Benjamin Harrison (23rd) "It is out of the Word of God that a system has come to make life sweet."

K. William McKinley (25th) "The more profoundly we study this wonderful Book . . . the better citizens we will become."

L. Theodore Roosevelt (26th) "No educated man can afford to be ignorant of the Bible."

M. Woodrow Wilson (28th) "The Bible is the one supreme source of revelation of the meaning of life."

N. Herbert Hoover (31st) "The whole of the inspirations of our civilization springs from the teachings of Christ . . . to read the Bible . . . is a necessity of American life."

O. Franklin D. Roosevelt (32nd) "It is a fountain of strength. . . . I feel that a comprehensive study of the Bible is a liberal education for anyone."

P. Dwight D. Eisenhower (34th) "In the highest sense the Bible is to us the unique repository of eternal spiritual truths."

II. From World Leaders—

A. William Gladstone—"I have known ninety-five great men of the world in my time, and of these, eighty-seven were followers of the Bible."

B. Winston Churchill—"We rest with assurance upon the impregnable rock of Holy Scripture."

C. Chiang Kai-Shek—"The Bible is the voice of the Holy Spirit."

D. Haile Selassie—"The Bible is not only a great book of historical reference, but it also is a guide for daily life, and for this reason I respect it and I love it."

E. Syngman Rhee—"Fellow prisoners held the Bible and turned the pages for me because my fingers were so crushed that I could not use them. I read the Bible, and I have read it the rest of my life."

III. From Generals—

A. Douglas MacArthur—"Believe me sir, never a night goes by, be I ever so tired, but I read the Word of God before I go to bed."

B. William K. Harrison—"The Bible is the Word of God, given by His inspiration for our use and benefit."

C. Robert E. Lee—"The Bible is a book in comparison with which all others in my eyes are of minor importance, and in which in all my perplexities and distresses has never failed to give me light and strength."

D. Stonewall Jackson—"God's promises change not . . . let us endeavor to adorn the doctrine of Christ in all things."

E. Oliver Cromwell—(Upon hearing Phil. 4:11-13 read as he lay dying) "He that was Paul's Christ is my Christ too."

IV. From Scientists—

A. Sir Isaac Newton—"We account the Scriptures of God to be the most sublime philosophy. I find more sure marks of authenticity in the Bible than in any profane history whatsoever."

B. Sir Francis Bacon—"The volume of Scriptures. . . . reveal the will of God."

C. Sir John Herschel—"All human discoveries seem to be made only for the purpose of confirming more and more strongly the truths come from on high and contained in the sacred writings. . . ."

D. Michael Faraday—"Why will people go astray when they have this blessed Book to guide them?"

E. James Dwight Dana—"Young men, as you go forth, remember that I, an old man, who has known only science all his life, say unto you that there is no truer facts than the facts found within the Holy Scriptures."

V. From Historians—

A. Arnold J. Toynbee—"It pierces through the Intellect and plays directly upon the heart."

B. H. G. Wells—"The Bible has been the Book that held together the fabric of Western civilization. . . . The civilization we possess could not come into existence and could not have been sustained without it."

C. Thomas Carlyle—"A Noble book! All men's book! . . . grand in its sincerity, in its simplicity, and in its epic melody."

VI. From Physicians—

A. Mark Hopkins—"Thus we have every conceivable species of historical proof, both external and internal. Thus do the very stones cry out."

B. Charles W. Mayo—"In sickness or in health, one can find comfort and constructive advice in the Bible."

VII. From Lawyers—

A. Daniel Webster—"I believe the Scriptures of the Old and New Testament to be the will and the Word of God."

B. Benjamin Franklin—"Young men, my advice to you is that you cultivate an acquaintance with, and a firm belief in, the Holy Scriptures."

C. Patrick Henry—"This is a Book worth more than all the others that were ever printed."

VIII. From Educators—

A. Timothy Dwight—"The Bible is a window in this prison-world through which we may look into eternity."

B. William Lyon Phelps—"Everyone who has a thorough knowledge of the Bible may truly be called educated . . . I believe knowledge of the Bible without a college course is more valuable than a college course without the Bible."

C. Henry Van Dyke—"No other book in the world has had such a strange vitality, such an outgoing power of influence and inspiration. . . . No man is poor or desolate who has this treasure for his own."

IX. From Philosophers & Writers—

A. Charles Dana—"Of all the books, the most indispensable and the most useful, the one whose knowledge is the most effective, is the Bible."

B. Horace Greeley—"It is impossible to mentally or socially enslave a Bible-reading people."

C. Immanuel Kant—"The existence of the Bible as a book for the people is the greatest benefit which the human race has ever experienced."

D. John Locke—"It has God for its Author, salvation for its end, and truth, without any mixture of error, for its matter: it is all pure, sincere, nothing too much, nothing wanting."

E. Count Leo Tolstoy—"Without the Bible the education of a child in the present state of society is impossible."

F. John Ruskin—"All I have taught in art, everything I have written, whatever greatness there has been in any thought of mine, whatever I have done in my life, has simply been due to the fact that, when I was a child, my mother daily read with me a part of the Bible, and daily made me learn a part of it by heart."

G. John Milton—"There are no songs like the songs of the Scriptures, no orations like the orations of the prophets."

H. William Cowper—"A Glory gilds the sacred page, Majestic like the sun: it gives a light to every age—it gives, but borrows none. . . ."

I. John Dryden—"It speaks no less than God in every line; Commanding words whose force is still the same. . . ."

J. Sir Walter Scott—"Within this awful volume lies the Mystery of mysteries."

K. Charles Dickens—"It is the best Book that ever was or ever will be in the world. . . ."

X. From Various Fields—

A. J. Edgar Hoover—"The Bible is the unfailing guide which points the way for men to the perfect life."

B. Bernard Baruch—"I have always placed the Bible as number one among the four books I think everyone should read and study. Therein one will find all the problems that beset mankind."

C. Helen Keller—"In the Bible I find a confidence mightier than the utmost evil. . . ."

D. Lowell Thomas—"The Bible is of vital importance in teaching freedom. . . ."

E. King George V—"The English Bible is . . . the most valuable thing that this world affords."

XI. From the Church Fathers—

A. Augustine—"Let us give in and yield our assent to the authority of Holy Scripture, which knows not how either to be deceived or to deceive. . . ."

B. John Chrysostom—"It is a great thing, this reading of the Scriptures! For it is not possible, I say, not possible ever to exhaust the minds of the Scriptures. It is a well which has no bottom."

C. Athanasius—"They were spoken and written by God through men who spoke of God. . . . Let no man add to these, neither let him take aught from these."

D. Origen—"For my part, I believe that not one jot or tittle of the divine instruction is in vain. We are never to say that there is anything impertinent or superfluous in the Scriptures of the Holy Spirit. . . ."

E. Jerome—"Give ear for a moment that I may tell you how you are to walk in the Holy Scriptures. All that we read in the Divine Book, while glistening and shining without, is yet far sweeter within."

F. Luther—"It cannot be otherwise, for the Scriptures are Divine; in them God speaks, and they are His Word. To hear or to read the Scriptures is nothing else than to hear God."

G. Calvin—"The Scriptures is the school of the Holy Spirit, in which, as nothing necessary and useful to be known is omitted, so nothing is taught which is not beneficial to know."

In concluding this section it may be necessary to stop here and consider some anticipated objections about all these "pious commercials" for the Bible. Some have felt the statements made by political persons, such as U.S. presidents, were made solely for election purposes, for, it is claimed, no atheist could ever be voted into the White House. But to say this is to deny the integrity of almost every American president. It should be also pointed out that many of these statements were made at a time when either the man was not a candidate for re-election, or had already moved out of the White House!

Furthermore, while history shows many famous "Bible haters" who later became "Bible lovers," it never records the opposite! To take this a step further, it can be shown that no evil and murderous dictator or tyrant in history was ever a friend of the Bible and that no good and wise leader was ever an enemy of God's Word! Thus to deny the authority of the Bible is to set oneself against practically every great leader in Western civilization! While it is true that this in itself constitutes no absolute proof of the Scriptures, it does, nevertheless, lend itself to Abraham Lincoln's famous proverb:

> You can fool some of the people all of the time, and all of the people some of the time, but you can't fool all of the people all of the time!

PART FOUR
Symbols for the Bible

I. A Mirror

For if any be a hearer of the word, and not a doer, he is like unto a man beholding his natural face in a glass: For he beholdeth himself, and goeth his way, and straightway forgetteth what manner of man he was. But whoso looketh into the perfect law of liberty, and continueth therein, he being not a forgetful hearer, but a doer of the work, this man shall be blessed in his deed (James 1:23-25).

It is called a mirror because it reflects the mind of God and the true condition of man.

II. A Seed

Being born again, not of corruptible seed, but of incorruptible, by the Word of God, which liveth and abideth forever (1 Pet. 1:23).

Of his own will begat He us with the Word of Truth, that we should be a kind of firstfruits of His Creatures (James 1:18).

Hear ye therefore the parable of the sower. When any one heareth the word of the kingdom, and understandeth it not, then cometh the wicked one, and catcheth away that which was sown in his heart. This is he which received seed by the way side. But he that received the seed into stony places, the same is he that heareth the word, and anon with joy receiveth it; Yet hath he not root in himself, but dureth for a while: for when tribulation or persecution ariseth because of the word, by and by he is offended. He also that received seed among the thorns is he that heareth the word; and the care of this world, and the deceitfulness of riches, choke the word, and he becometh unfruitful. But he that received seed into the good ground is he that heareth the word, and understandeth it; which also beareth fruit, and bringeth forth, some an hundredfold, some sixty, some thirty (Matt. 13:18-23).

It is called a seed because, once properly planted, it brings forth life, growth, and fruit.

III. Water

> Husbands, love your wives, even as Christ also loved the church, and gave himself for it; That he might sanctify and cleanse it with the washing of water by the word, That he might present it to himself a glorious church, not having spot, or wrinkle, or any such thing; but that it should be holy and without blemish (Eph. 5:25-27).

It is called water because of its cleansing, quenching, and refreshing qualities. (See Ps. 119:9; 42:1; Prov. 25:25; Isa. 55: 10; Heb. 10:22; Rev. 22:17.)

IV. A Lamp

> Thy word is a lamp unto my feet, and a light unto my path (Ps. 119: 105).

> For the commandment is a lamp; and the law is light; and reproofs of instruction are the way of life (Prov. 6:23).

> We have also a more sure word of prophecy; whereunto ye do well that ye take heed, as unto a light that shineth in a dark place, until the day dawn, and the day star arise in your hearts (2 Pet. 1:19).

It is called a lamp because it shows us where we are now, it guides us in the next step, and it keeps us from falling.

V. A Sword

> For the word of God is quick, and powerful, and sharper than any twoedged sword, piercing even to the dividing asunder of soul and spirit, and of the joints and marrow, and is a discerner of the thoughts and intents of the heart (Heb. 4:12).

> And take the helmet of salvation, and the sword of the Spirit, which is the word of God (Eph. 6:17).

It is called a sword because of its piercing ability, operating with equal effectiveness upon sinners, saints and Satan! Of the various armour pieces mentioned in Eph. 6:11-17, all to be worn by the believer, the only offensive piece is the "sword of the Spirit, which is the Word of God."

VI. Precious Metals

A. Gold—Ps. 19:10; 119:127

B. Silver—Ps. 12:6

> Therefore I love thy commandments above gold; yea above fine gold (Ps. 119:127).

> The words of the Lord are pure words: as silver tried in a furnace of earth, purified seven times (Ps. 12:6).

It is referred to as precious metals because of its desirability, its preciousness, its beauty, and its value.

VII. Nourishing Food

A. Milk

> As newborn babes, desire the sincere milk of the word, that ye may grow thereby (1 Pet. 2:2).

B. Meat

> For when for the time ye ought to be teachers, ye have need that one teach you again which be the first principles of the oracles of God; and are become such as have need of milk, and not of strong meat. For every one that useth milk is unskilful in the word of righteousness; for he is a babe. But strong meat belongeth to them that are of full age, even those who by reason of use have their senses exercised to discern both good and evil (Heb. 5:12-14).

C. Bread

> I am the living bread which came down from heaven: if any man eat of this bread, he shall live for ever: and the bread that I will give is my flesh, which I will give for the life of the world (John 6:51).

D. Honey

> More to be desired are they than gold, yea, than much fine gold: sweeter also than honey and the honeycomb (Ps. 19:10).

It is referred to as nourishing food because of the strength it imparts. The Bible is the original "soul food."

VIII. A Hammer

> Is not my word like as a fire? saith the Lord; and like a hammer that breaketh the rock in pieces (Jer. 23:29)?

It is referred to as a hammer because of its ability to both tear down and to build up! (See Acts 9:4; Jude 1:20.)

IX. A Fire

> Then I said, I will not make mention of him, nor speak any more in his name. But his word was in mine heart as a burning fire shut up in my bones, and I was weary with forbearing, and I could not stay (Jer. 20:9).
>
> And they said one to another, Did not our heart burn within us, while he talked with us by the way, and while he opened to us the scriptures (Luke 24:32).

It is called a fire because of its judging, purifying, and consuming abilities.

PART FIVE

The Supreme Authority of the Bible

Perhaps the grandest and most conclusive description of the Bible was penned by the apostle Paul in a letter to a young pastor. Here he wrote:

> And that from a child thou hast known the holy scriptures, which are able to make thee wise unto salvation through faith which is in Christ Jesus. All scripture is given by inspiration of God, and is profitable for doctrine, for reproof, for correction, for instruction in righteousness: That the man of God may be perfect, thoroughly furnished unto all good works (2 Tim. 3:15-17).

In this remarkable passage Paul claims the Bible is profitable—

1. for *doctrine*—that is, it may be used as the perfect textbook to present the systematic teachings of the great truths relating to God Himself.
2. for *reproof*—that is, the Bible is to be used to convict us of the wrong in our lives.
3. for *correction*—that is, it will then show us the right way.
4. for *instruction in righteousness*—that is, God's Word provides all the necessary details which will allow a Christian to become fully equipped for every good work!

Because of all this, the Bible rightly demands absolute and sole authority over any other source in the life of the child of God. This authority would exceed that of the following:

I. Over Human Reason

God gave us our minds and desires that we should use them! This is seen in two classic passages, one directed to the unsaved, the other to the saved.

> Come now, and let us reason together, saith the Lord; though your sins be as scarlet, they shall be as white as snow; though they be red like crimson, they shall be as wool (Isa. 1:18).

> I beseech you therefore, brethren, by the mercies of God, that ye present your bodies a living sacrifice, holy, acceptable unto God, which is your reasonable service. And be not conformed to this

> world: but be ye transformed by the renewing of your mind, that ye may prove what is that good, and acceptable, and perfect, will of God (Rom. 12:1-2).

However, there are times when God desires us to submit our human reasoning to Him. Note the following admonition:

> Trust in the Lord with all thine heart; and lean not unto thine own understanding. In all thy ways acknowledge him, and he shall direct thy paths. Be not wise in thine own eyes: fear the Lord, and depart from evil (Prov. 3:5-7).

Often our reasoning is as the thinking of Naaman, who when asked to take a seven-fold bath in Jordan's muddy waters, angrily replied:

> Behold, I thought, He will surely come out to me, and stand, and call on the name of the Lord his God, and strike his hand over the place, and recover the leper (2 Kings 5:11).

But Elisha did not do so! Often God's ways are different from our ways.

> For my thoughts are not your thoughts, neither are your ways my ways, saith the Lord. For as the heavens are higher than the earth, so are my ways higher than your ways, and my thoughts than your thoughts (Isa. 55:8-9).

II. Over the Church

The New Testament abounds with passages which declare Christ is the Head of the Church! (See Eph. 1:22; 2:19-20; 4:15-16; 5:23-30; Col. 1:18; 2:9.) The Saviour, it must be remembered, gave birth to the Church, and not the other way around. (See Matt. 16:18.) Thus the Christian must look to the Bible and not to any earthly church for final instruction. Sometimes even those local churches mentioned in the Bible itself were grievously wrong. Note the following description of New Testament churches, some of which were started by Paul himself!

A. The Church at Ephesus

> Nevertheless I have somewhat against thee, because thou hast left thy first love. Remember therefore from whence thou art fallen, and repent, and do the first works; or else I will come unto thee quickly, and will remove thy candlestick out of his place, except thou repent (Rev. 2:4-5).

B. The Church at Pergamos

> But I have a few things against thee, because thou hast there them that hold the doctrine of Balaam, who taught Balac to cast a stumblingblock before the children of Israel, to eat things sacrificed unto idols, and to commit fornication. So hast thou also them that hold the doctrine of the Nicolaitanes, which thing I hate. Repent: or else I will come unto thee quickly, and will fight against them with the sword of my mouth (Rev. 2:14-16).

C. The Church at Thyatira

> Notwithstanding I have a few things against thee, because thou sufferest that woman Jezebel, which calleth herself a prophetess, to teach and to seduce my servants to commit fornication, and to eat things sacrificed unto idols (Rev. 2:20).

D. The Church at Sardis

> And unto the angel of the church in Sardis write: These things saith he that hath the seven Spirits of God, and the seven stars; I know thy works, that thou hast a name that thou livest, and art dead. Be watchful, and strengthen the things which remain, that are ready to die: For I have not found thy works perfect before God. Remember therefore how thou hast received and heard, and hold fast, and repent. If therefore thou shalt not watch, I will come on thee as a thief, and thou shalt not know what hour I will come upon thee (Rev. 3:1-3).

E. The Church at Laodicea

> I know thy works, that thou art neither cold nor hot. I would thou wert cold or hot. So then because thou art lukewarm, and neither cold nor hot, I will spue thee out of my mouth. Because thou sayest, I am rich, and increased with goods, and have need of nothing; and knowest not that thou art wretched, and miserable, and poor, and blind, and naked: I counsel thee to buy of me gold tried in the fire, that thou mayest be rich; and white raiment, that thou mayest be clothed, and that the shame of thy nakedness do not appear; and anoint thine eyes with eyeslave, that thou mayest see. As many as I love, I rebuke and chasten: be zealous therefore and repent (Rev. 3:15-19).

III. Over Tradition

In this atomic and space age in which we live today where change occurs at rocket speed, it will doubtless cause many to appreciate even more some of our beautiful traditions of the past. And rightly so! But traditions, like changes, can be wrong! If a thing was in error when it began, it is still in error regardless of the centuries that separate it from us today. Often in the past, hurtful "traditions of the fathers" have crept into the Church of the Living God. Our Saviour Himself was grieved over some harmful Jewish traditions. Note His words:

> And honour not his father or his mother, he shall be free. Thus have ye made the commandment of God of none effect by your tradition (Matt. 15:6).

Later Paul would warn also of this.

> Beware lest any man spoil you through philosophy and vain deceit, after the tradition of men, after the rudiments of the world, and not after Christ (Col. 2:8).

IV. Over Popes and Preachers

Only recently a well-known protestant "faith healer" died in a lonely motel in Los Angeles County, California. A coroner's report revealed he died of sclerosis of the liver, caused by acute alcoholism. It was then revealed the man had been an alcoholic for many years.

Who does not know other examples of this tragic story? The most godly pastors are, after all, only finite men fully capable (apart from God's grace) of the vilest sins! This is also true of popes as well. In his Bible handbook, Dr. H. H. Halley lists the following information concerning some of the early popes in history:

A. Sergius III—(904-911)

He lived with a notorious harlot, Marozia, and they raised their illegitimate children to become popes and cardinals. This period is known as "the Rule of the Harlots."

B. John X—(914-928)

He was smothered to death by Marozia, as she disapproved of his reign.

C. John XII—(955-963)

He was a grandson of Marozia, and was guilty of almost every crime. He violated virgins and widows, lived with his father's mistress, made the papal palace a brothel, and was killed in the very act of adultery by the woman's enraged husband!

D. Boniface VIII—(1012-1024)

He murdered Pope John XIV to get on the throne.

E. Benedict IX—(1033-1045)

He was made a pope as a boy of twelve. He committed murders and adulteries in broad daylight, robbed graves, and was finally driven out of Rome by enraged citizens!

F. Gregory VI—(1046)

He was one of three rivals for the throne at this time. Rome swarmed with hired assassins, as each pope was trying to cut the throat of the other two. Finally, Emperor Henry III stepped in, kicked all three out, and appointed his own pope, Clement II.

G. Innocent II—(1198-1216)

He was the most powerful of all popes—and anything but innocent! He condemned England's *Magna Charta,* and forbade Bible reading.

H. John XXIII—(1410-1415)

He was called by some the most depraved criminal who ever lived. Was guilty of almost every known crime. As a cardinal, some 200 maidens, nuns, and married women fell victims to his lust. As pope he intensified this, lived in adultery with his brother's wife, was guilty of sodomy, and openly denied any eternal life.

I. Pius II—(1458-1464)

He spoke openly of the methods he used to seduce women, encouraged young men to do the same, and even offered to instruct them in sexual perversions!

J. Alexander VI—(1492-1503)

He loved to give big suppers at the palace, during which he would poison wealthy cardinals and seize their estates. However, he accidentally poisoned himself by drinking wine meant for another churchman!

Before concluding this section, let us consider a quotation from the book, *The Other Side of Rome,* by John B. Wilder.

One of the most deplorable scenes ever enacted on the stage of human events was the trial and treatment accorded Pope Formosus. I found this record in Dwight Sedwick's *A Short History of Italy,* but it is also given, in much the same detail, in *The Catholic Encyclopedia.* The strange element in this case was the fact that Pope Formosus was brought to trial several months after his death. This pope had made an unfortunate political blunder during his reign as head of the Catholic Church. He invited the King of Germany to visit Rome and be crowned Emperor of Germany. It so happened that this particular king was unpopular with important elements in the College of Cardinals. Bitter resentment was held against Formosus when he moved to elevate the German monarch to the title of emperor. Formosus went ahead with the Coronation, but he died shortly after the affair. The Cardinals elected a new pope from the faction that had so bitterly opposed Formosus when he was Pope. The new pope called a meeting of the Cardinals and bishops and formed a synod. That made these men the highest spiritual tribunal on earth. Formal charges were filed against the dead Formosus, and he was summoned to appear before this lofty assembly. What follows is a horror story. The pope had lain in his grave for several months, but at the summons, his body was dug up and brought to the chambers of the great synod. There it was dressed in all the rich trappings of the papacy. The crown of Rome was pressed upon the loose scalp of the corpse, and the honored scepter of the Holy Office was placed in the stiff fingers of his rotting hand. The dead man was propped upon the throne and the trial began. Lawyers were appointed to represent him, but the new pope himself assumed the responsibilities of the prosecution. The new pope stepped forward and closely questioned the dead man. But Formosus did not reply. If he had replied, the probabilities are that the synod would have been dissolved at that moment. It did not take long to find Formosus guilty, since he made no effort to defend himself. He was found guilty of violating the Canons of the church, and all his acts as pope were declared null and void! Then he was degraded. His bright robes were ripped from his body, and the crown snatched from his silent skull, and the scepter torn from the stiff fingers that held it. The three fingers used in bestowing the pontifical blessing were hacked off his decaying hand, and his body was thrown out into the street. It was tied behind a cart and dragged about the streets of the city until finally it was cast into the Tiber River." [7]

V. Over Feelings and Experiences

At times Christians fall unto error because they "felt led" to do or say certain things. However we must learn that at times our feelings can be treacherous and totally untrustworthy. The psalmist often spoke of this:

> I had fainted, unless I had believed to see the goodness of the Lord in the Land of the living (Ps. 27:13).

> Why art thou cast down, O my soul? and why art thou disquieted in me? hope thou in God: For I shall yet praise him for the help of his countenance (Ps. 42:5).

> I cried unto God with my voice, even unto God with my voice; and he gave ear unto me. In the day of my trouble I sought the Lord: my sore ran in the night, and ceased not: my soul refused to be comforted. I remembered God, and was troubled: I complained, and my spirit was overwhelmed. Thou holdest mine eyes waking: I am so troubled that I cannot speak. I have considered the days of old, the years of ancient times. I call to remembrance my song in the night: I commune with mine own heart: and my spirit made diligent search. Will the Lord cast off for ever? and will he be favourable no more? Is his mercy clean gone for ever? doth his promise fail for evermore? Hath God forgotten to be gracious? hath he in anger shut up his tender mercies? And I said, this is my infirmity: But I will remember the years of the right hand of the most High (Ps. 77:1-10).

> I said in my haste, All men are liars (Ps. 116:11).

This is not only the case with our feelings, but also our experiences. One of Job's three "friends," Eliphaz, based all his advice to the suffering Job on experience (Job 4:12-16). He is later severely rebuked by God Himself for doing this (See Job 42:7).

Thus as valuable as personal experience may be, it is no substitute for the revealed Word of God!

A list has been compiled showing the various functions of this authoritative Book called the Bible.

A. It upholds—Ps. 119:116
B. It orders steps—119:133
C. It produces joy—119:162
D. It strengthens—119:28; 1 John 2:14
E. It gives hope—119:74, 81
F. It gives light—119:105, 130
G. It gives understanding—119:169
H. It shows God's will—Isa. 55:11
I. It builds up—Acts 20:32
J. It produces fruit—John 15:7

K. It convicts of sin—Heb. 4:12
L. It converts the soul—James 1:18; 1 Pet. 1:23
M. It cleanses the conscience—John 15:3
N. It consecrates life—John 17:17
O. It corrects the wrong—2 Tim. 3:16
P. It confirms the right—John 8:31
Q. It comforts the heart—Ps. 119:50, 54

Because of this, the child of God is to respond to this authoritative Book in the following ways:

A. Read it—Col. 3:16; Deut. 31:11; Rev. 1:3; Isa. 34:16; Luke 4:16; Eph. 3:4; 1 Thess. 5:27; 2 Tim. 4:13; Col. 4:1.
B. Heed it—Ps. 119:9; 1 Tim. 4:16.
C. Seed it—Matt. 28:19, 20.
D. Desire it—1 Pet. 2:2.
E. Preach it—2 Tim. 4:2.
F. Rightly divide it—2 Tim. 2:15.
G. Live by it—Matt. 4:4.
H. Use it—Eph. 6:17.
I. Suffer for it, and if need be, to die for it—Rev. 1:9; 6:9; 20:4.

The Child of God is to KNOW it in his head, STOW it in his heart, SHOW it in his life, and SOW it in the world.

See also the following Scriptures:

Deut. 4:1-10; 12:32; Josh. 1:8; Ps. 33:6; Prov. 30:5, 6; Mark 4:24; Luke 8:12; John 12:48-50; Heb. 1:1-3; 2:1-4; Rev. 1:1-3; 20:12; 22:18, 19; Rom. 8:7; 1 Cor. 2:14.

Thus the authority of God's Word is as a STETHESCOPE, for it probes within, as a MICROSCOPE, for it looks upon, and as a TELESCOPE, as it sees beyond!

PART SIX

How the Sixty-Six Books of the Bible Were Collected

I. The Writing Materials of the Bible

The Spirit of God moved upon the authors of the Bible to record their precious messages upon whatever object was in current use at the time of the writing. Thus once again we see the marvelous condescension of God! These writing materials would include:

A. Clay—Jer. 17:13; Ezek. 4:1.

B. Stone—Exod. 24:12; 31:18; 32:15-16; 34:1, 28; Deut. 5:22; 27:2-3; Josh. 8:31-32.

C. Papyrus—(made by pressing and gluing two layers of split papyrus reeds together in order to form a sheet)—Rev. 5:1; 2 John 12.

D. Vellum (calf skin), Parchment (lamb skin), Leather (cowhide). See 2 Tim. 4:13.

E. Metal—Exod. 28:36; Job 19:24; Matt. 22:19-20.

II. The Language of the Bible

A. The Old Testament was written in Hebrew, with the following exceptions appearing in Aramaic. These are: Ezra 4:8–6:18; 7:12-26; Dan. 2:4–7:28; Jer. 10:11. Why did God choose Hebrew? In their book *A General Introduction to the Bible,* authors Geisler and Nix note the following:

> It is a pictorial language, speaking with vivid, bold metaphors which challenge and dramatize the story. The Hebrew language possesses a facility to present "pictures" of the events narrated. "The Hebrew thought in pictures, and consequently his nouns are concrete and vivid. There is no such thing as neuter gender, for the Semite everything is alive. Compound words are lacking. . . . There is no wealth of adjectives . . ." The language shows "vast powers of association and, therefore, of imagination." Some of this is lost in the English translation, but even so, "much of the vivid, concrete, and forthright character of our English Old Testament is really a carrying over into English of something of

> the genius of the Hebrew tongue." As a pictorial language, Hebrew presents a vivid picture of the acts of God among a people who became examples or illustrations for future generations (cf. 1 Cor. 10:11). Since the Old Testament was intended to be presented graphically in a 'picture-language.'
>
> Further, Hebrew is a personal language. It addresses itself to the heart and emotions rather than merely to the mind or reason. Sometimes even nations are given personalities (cf. Mal. 1:2-3). Always the appeal is to the person in the concrete realities of life and not to the abstract or theoretical. Hebrew is a language through which the message is felt rather than thought. As such, the language was highly qualified to convey to the individual believer as well as to the worshiping community the personal relation of the living God in the events of the Jewish nation. It was much more qualified to record the realization of revelation in the life of a nation than to propositionalize that revelation for the propagation among all nations.[8]

B. The entire New Testament was written in Greek. Again, to quote from Geisler and Nix:

> Greek was an intellectual language. It was more a language of the mind than of the heart, a fact to which the great Greek philosophers gave abundant evidence. Greek was more suited to codifying a communication or reflecting on a revelation of God in order to put it into simple communicable form. It was a language that could more easily render the credible into the intelligible than could Hebrew. It was for this reason that New Testament Greek was a most useful medium for expressing the propositional truth of the New Testament, as Hebrew was for expressing the biographical truth of the Old Testament. Since Greek possessed a technical precision not found in Hebrew, the theological truths which were more generally expressed in the Hebrew of the Old Testament were more precisely formulated in the Greek of the New Testament.
>
> Furthermore, Greek was a nearly universal language. The truth of God in the Old Testament, which was initially revealed to one nation (Israel), was appropriately recorded in the language of the nation (Hebrew). But the fuller revelation given by God in the New Testament was not restricted in that way. In the words of Luke's gospel, the message of Christ was to "be preached in his name to all nations" (Luke 24:47). The language most appropriate for the propagation of this message was naturally the one that was most widely spoken throughout the world. Such was the

common (Koine) Greek, a thoroughly international language of the first century Mediterranean world.

It may be concluded, then, that God chose the very languages to communicate His truth which had, in His providence, been prepared to express most effectively the kind of truth He desired at that particular time, in the unfolding of His overall plan. Hebrew, with its pictorial and personal vividness, expressed well the biographical truth of the Old Testament. Greek, with its intellectual and universal potentialities, served well for the doctrinal and evangelistic demands of the New Testament.[9]

III. The Reason for the Writing of the Bible

Perhaps the one supreme difference between man and all other creatures (apart from his immortal soul, of course), is his God-given ability to express his thoughts on paper. It has been observed that while it was no doubt desirable to speak *to* the prophets "in divers manners" in time past, the best way to communicate with *all* men of *all* ages is through the written record! The advantages of the written method are many, of course:

A. Precision—One's thoughts must be somewhat precise to be written.

B. Propagation—The most accurate way to communicate a message is usually through writing.

C. Preservation—Men die, and memories fail, but the written record remains! It may be said the New Testament especially was written for the following reasons:

1. Because of the demands of the early Church—1 Thess. 5:27; 1 Tim. 4:13; 2 Tim. 3:16-17.
2. Because of false doctrines (to counteract it).
3. Because of missionary endeavors (to propagate it).
4. Because of persecution and politics.

IV. The Old Testament

A. The order of the books in the Hebrew Old Testament—The thirty-nine books in our English Old Testament appear somewhat differently in a present-day Hebrew Bible. They cover the identical material but number twenty-four and are arranged in a three-fold division. This division is:

1. The Law (Torah)
   a. Genesis
   b. Exodus
   c. Leviticus
   d. Numbers
   e. Deuteronomy

2. The Prophets (Nebhiim)

   a. Former Prophets—4 books:
      (1) Joshua
      (2) Judges
      (3) Samuel
      (4) Kings

   b. Latter Prophets—(Major and Minor sections)
   Major Sections—
      (1) Isaiah
      (2) Jeremiah
      (3) Ezekiel

   c. *Minor Section*
      (1) Hosea
      (2) Joel
      (3) Amos
      (4) Obadiah
      (5) Jonah
      (6) Micah
      (7) Nahum
      (8) Habakkuk
      (9) Zephaniah
      (10) Haggai
      (11) Zechariah
      (12) Malachi

3. The Writings

   a. The poetical books (3)
      (1) Psalms
      (2) Proverbs
      (3) Job

   b. The Scrolls (5)
      (1) Song of Solomon
      (2) Ruth
      (3) Lamentations
      (4) Ecclesiastes
      (5) Esther

   c. Prophetic—Historical (3)

(1) Daniel
(2) Ezra—Nehemiah
(3) Chronicles

B. The suggested order of the writings

Many believe the book of Job to be the oldest in the Word of God. It may well have been written as early as 2000 B.C. One of the earliest parts certainly to have been written was that section found in Exodus 17. This occurred on Israel's route to Palestine. Joshua had just won a tremendous victory over a fierce desert tribe called the Amalekites. After the battle was over we read:

> And the Lord said unto Moses, Write this for a memorial in a book, and release it in the ears of Joshua: for I will utterly put out the remembrance of Amalek from under heaven (Exod. 17:14).

Other early sections of the Word of God would of course include the Law of Moses. (See Deut. 31:24-26.) The following is but a mere suggestion of the writing of the Old Testament books:

1. Job—2150 B.C.
2. Pentateuch—1402 B.C.
3. Joshua—before 1350 B.C.
4. Judges and Ruth—before 1050 B.C.
5. Psalms—before 965 B.C.
6. Proverbs, Ecclesiastes, Song of Solomon—before 926 B.C.
7. First & Second Samuel—before 926 B.C.
8. First Kings and First Chronicles—before 848 B.C.
9. Obadiah—848 B.C.
10. Joel—835 B.C.
11. Jonah—780 B.C.
12. Amos—765 B.C.
13. Hosea—755 B.C.
14. Isaiah—750 B.C.
15. Micah—740 B.C.
16. Jeremiah & Lamentations—640 B.C.
17. Nahum—630 B.C.
18. Habakkuk & Zephaniah—625 B.C.

19. Ezekiel—593 B.C.
20. Second Kings & Second Chronicles—before 539 B.C.
21. Daniel—before 538 B.C.
22. Haggai & Zechariah—520 B.C.
23. Esther—after 476 B.C.
24. Ezra—after 458 B.C.
25. Nehemiah—after 445 B.C.
26. Malachi—432 B.C.

C. The location of the Old Testament books

1. Before the Babylonian Captivity

Prior to this period (606 B.C.) the Old Testament books were apparently laid beside the Ark of the Covenant in the Temple. This is indicated in the following passages:

> And Moses came and told the people all the words of the Lord, and all the judgments; and all the people answered with one voice, and said, All the words which the Lord hath said will we do. And Moses wrote all the words of the Lord, and rose up early in the morning, and builded an altar under the hill, and twelve pillars, according to the twelve tribes of Israel. . . . And he took the book of the covenant, and read in the audience of the people: and they said, All that the Lord hath said will we do, and be obedient (Exod. 24:3, 4, 7).

> And it came to pass, when Moses had made an end of writing the words of this law in a book, until they were finished, That Moses commanded the Levites, which bare the ark of the covenant of the Lord, saying, Take this book of the law, and put it in the side of the ark of the covenant of the Lord your God, that it may be there for a witness against thee (Deut. 31:24-26).

> And Hilkiah the high priest said unto Shaphan the scribe, I have found the book of the law in the house of the Lord. And Hilkiah gave the book to Shaphan, and he read it. And Shaphan the scribe came to the king, and brought the king word again, and said, Thy servants have gathered the money that was found in the house, and have delivered it into the hand of them that do the work, that have the oversight of the house of the Lord. And Shaphan the scribe shewed the king, saying Hilkiah the priest hath delivered me a book. And Shaphan read it before the king (2 Kings 22:8-10).

> So Joshua made a covenant with the people that day, and set them a statute and an ordinance in Shechem. And Joshua wrote these words in the book of the law of God, and took a great stone, and set it up there under an oak, that was by the sanctuary of the Lord (Josh. 24:25-26).

> Then Samuel told the people the manner of the kingdom, and wrote it in a book, and laid it up before the Lord. And Samuel sent all the people away, every man to his house (1 Sam. 10:25).

2. During the Babylonian Captivity

The books were probably carried to Babylon and later collected by Daniel. In 9:2 of his book, the prophet Daniel writes:

> In the first year of his reign I Daniel understood by books the number of the years, whereof the word of the Lord came to Jeremiah the prophet that he would accomplish seventy years in the desolations of Jerusalem.

Here Daniel specifically states he was reading Jeremiah and "the books," a reference no doubt to the other Old Testament books written up to that time.

3. After the Babylonian Captivity

These books may have been taken back to Jerusalem by Ezra the prophet and kept in the newly-completed temple. (See Ezra 3:10-11; 6:15-18; Neh. 8:1-8.)

V. The New Testament

The New Testament was written over a period of about fifty years (approximately 50-100 A.D.), by eight separate authors.

A. A suggested chronological order and possible dating of the New Testament books.

1. James—49 A.D. (written from Jerusalem)
2. First and Second Thessalonians—52 A.D. (written from Corinth)
3. First Corinthians—55 A.D. (written from Macedonia)
4. Second Corinthians—56 A.D. (written from Macedonia)
5. Galatians—57 A.D. (written from Ephesus)
6. Romans—58 A.D. (written from Corinth)
7. Luke—59 A.D. (written from Caesarea)

8. Acts—60 A.D. (written from Rome)
9. Philippians, Colossians, Ephesians, Philemon—61, 62 A.D. (written from Rome)
10. Matthew—63 A.D. (written from Judea)
11. Mark—63 A.D. (written from Rome)
12. Hebrews—64 A.D. (written from Jerusalem)
13. First Timothy—65 A.D. (written from Macedonia)
14. First Peter—65 A.D. (written from Babylon)
15. Second Peter—66 A.D. (unknown)
16. Titus—66 A.D. (written from Greece)
17. Jude—67 A.D. (unknown)
18. Second Timothy—67 A.D. (written from Rome)
19. Gospel of John—85-90 A.D. (written from Ephesus)
20. First John—90-95 A.D. (written from Judea)
21. Second and Third John—90-95 A.D. (written from
22. Revelation—90-95 A.D. (written from Isle of Patmos)

B. The number of the writers—

1. Matthew—author of Matthew
2. Mark—author of Mark
3. Luke—author of Luke and Acts
4. John—author of John, First, Second, Third John and Revelation
5. James—author of James
6. Jude—author of Jude
7. Peter—author of First and Second Peter
8. Paul—author of fourteen remaining New Testament epistles

VI. The Determination of the Canon

A. The tests given to the biblical books

Various books of the Bible, especially those of the New Testament, were submitted to certain rigid tests by the early Church. These tests included:

1. Authorship—Who wrote the book or the epistle?

2. Local church acceptance—Had it been read by the various churches? What was their opinion?

3. Church Fathers' recognition—Had the pupils of the disciples quoted from the book? As an example, a man named Polycarp was a disciple of John the apostle. Therefore one test of a book might be "What did Polycarp think of it?"

4. Book subject matter content—What did the book teach? Did it contradict other recognized books?

5. Personal edification—Did the book have the ability to inspire, convict, and edify local congregations and individual believers?

In closing this section it should be stated it was a combination of these five steps, and not just one alone, which helped determine whether a book was inspired or not. Contrary to what may have seemed vital, canonicity was *not* determined at all by either the age or the language of a given book. For example, there were many ancient books mentioned in the Old Testament (see Num. 21:14; Josh. 10:3) which were not in the Old Testament canon. Also, some of the apocryphal books (such as Tobit) were written in Hebrew but were not included in the Old Testament, while some books (like portions of Daniel) written in Aramaic were included in the canon!

B. The writings that were unacceptable

After the Old Testament canon had been recognized by the Jews as being officially closed, and prior to the New Testament period, there arose a section of literature called the Apocrypha. This word literally means "that which is hidden" and consists of fourteen books.

1. The contents of the Apocrypha

a. First Esdros—Covers much of the material found in Ezra, Nehemiah, and second Chronicles. But it also includes a fanciful story concerning three Jewish servants in Persia. They were all asked a question by King Darius concerning what was the greatest thing in the world. One said wine, another replied women, while the third claimed truth was. He won, and when offered a reward, suggested the King allow the Jews to rebuild the temple in Jerusalem.

b. Second Esdros—Contains certain visions given to Ezra dealing with God's government of the world and the restoration of certain lost Scriptures.

c. Tobit—The story of a pious Jew (Tobit) who is accidentally blinded (by sparrow dung) and is later healed by an angel named Raphael who applies a concoction of fish heart, liver, and gall to his eye.

d. Judith—The story of a beautiful and devout Jewish princess who saves Jerusalem from being destroyed by Nebuchadnezzar's invading armies. This she does by beguiling the enemy general through her beauty, then returning to Jerusalem with his head in her handbag!

e. The remainder of Esther—There are additional inserts to this book to show the hand of God in the narrative by putting the word "God" in the text. The word God does not appear in the Old Testament book of Esther.

f. The wisdom of Solomon—This book has been called "The Gem of the Apocrypha," and is one of the loftier books of the Apocrypha.

g. Ecclesiastes—Also called "the Wisdom of Jews, the Son of Sirach." It resembles the book of Proverbs, and gives rules for personal conduct in all details of civil, religious, and domestic life.

h. First Maccabees—This historical account on the Maccabean period relates events of the Jews' heroic struggle for liberty (175-135 B.C.)

i. Second Maccabees—This work covers in part the same period as First Maccabees but is somewhat inferior content-wise.

j. Baruch—Supposedly written by Jeremiah's secretary, Baruch. It contains prayers and confessions of the Jews in exile, with promises of restoration.

k. The Song of the three children—Inserted in the book of Daniel, right after the fiery furnace episode (Dan. 3: 23). It contains an eloquent prayer of Azariah, one of the three Hebrew men thrown in the fire.

l. The story of Susanna—A story relating how the godly wife of a wealthy Jew in Babylon, falsely accused of adultery, was cleared by the wisdom of Daniel.

m. Bel and the Dragon—This is also added to the book of Daniel. The book contains two stories:

(1) The first concerns how Daniel proves to the King his great idol god Bel is a dead idol, and that the Bel priests are religious crooks.

(2) Unger's Handbook describes this event in the following words:

> The other legend concerns a dragon worshiped in Babylon. Daniel, summoned to do it homage, feeds it a mixture of pitch, hair, and fat, which causes it to explode. The enraged populace compels the King to throw Daniel in the den of lions where he is fed on the sixth day by the prophet Habakkuk, who is angelically transported to Babylon by the hair of his head while carrying food and drink to the reapers in Judea. On the seventh day the King rescues Daniel and throws his would-be destroyers to the hungry lions.[10]

n. The Prayer of Manasses—This is the supposed confessional prayer of wicked King Manasseh, of Judah, after he was carried away prisoner to Babylon by the Assyrians.

2. Reasons for rejecting the Apocrypha—"Why don't you Protestants have all the books of the Bible in your King James Version?" Often Christians and Bible lovers are confronted with this question by those who have accepted the Apocrypha into their translations of the Bible. Why indeed do we *not* include these fourteen books? There are many sound scriptural reasons for not doing this.

a. The Apocrypha was never included in the Old Testament canon by such recognized authorities as the Pharisees, Ezra the prophet, etc.

b. It was never quoted by either Jews or any other New Testament writers.

c. The great Jewish historian Josephus excluded it.

d. The well-known Jewish philosopher Philo did not recognize it.

e. The early Church Fathers excluded it.

f. The Bible translator Jerome did not accept them as inspired, although he was forced by the Pope to include them into the Latin Vulgate Bible.

g. None of the fourteen books claim divine inspiration; in fact, some actually disclaim it!

h. Some books contain historical and geographical errors.

i. Some books teach false doctrine, such as praying for the dead.

j. No Apocrypha book can be found in any catalogue list of canonical books composed during the first four centuries A.D. In fact, it was not until 1596 at the Council of Trent that the Roman Catholic Church officially recognized these books, basically in an attempt to strengthen their position, which had been grievously weakened by the great reformer Martin Luther.

C. Some canonical books were at first doubted but later fully accepted. During the first few years of early Church history there were some twelve biblical books which were temporarily objected to for various reasons. These were:

1. Old Testament Books

a. The Song of Solomon—because it seemed to some to be a mere poem on human love.

b. Ecclesiastes—because some felt it taught atheism! (See 9:5.)

c. Esther—because it did not mention the word "God" in the entire book.

d. Ezekiel—because it seemed to contradict the Mosaic Law.

e. Proverbs—because it seemed to contradict itself! (See Prov. 26:4-5.)

2. New Testament Books

a. Hebrews—because of the uncertainty about the book's authorship.

b. James—because it seemed to contradict the teachings of Paul. (Compare James 2:20 with Eph. 2:8-9.)

c. Second and Third John—because they seemed to be simply two personal letters.

d. Jude—because the author refers to an uncanonical Old Testament book, the book of Enoch.

e. Revelation—because of the uncertainty about the book's authorship and because of its many mysterious symbols.

VII. The Finalization of the Canon

A. The Old Testament

By the year 300 B.C. (at the latest) all Old Testament books had been written, collected, revered, and recognized as official, canonical books. Many believe Ezra the prophet led the first recognition council.

B. The New Testament

During the Third Council of Carthage, held in 397 A.D., the twenty-seven New Testament books were declared to be canonical. However, it absolutely *must* be understood that the Bible is NOT an authorized collection of books, but rather a collection of authorized books. In other words, the twenty-seven New Testament books were not inspired because the Carthage Council proclaimed them to be, but rather the Council proclaimed them to be such because they were already inspired.

PART SEVEN

Important Historical Translations of the Bible:

Perhaps the most thrilling story in mankind's history is the true account of the earnest (and sometimes agonizing) efforts to translate God's precious Word in the language of a particular day. Literally billions of intensive man-hours have been spent doing this. We shall now briefly examine some of the better-known fruits of all this sweat and study.

I. Publications up to the time of Jesus

A. The Dead Sea Scrolls

During 1947, in a series of caves near the Dead Sea, a discovery was made that would soon excite the entire religious world. These were the Dead Sea Scrolls. Dr. William F. Albright states this find was "the most important discovery ever made concerning the Old Testament manuscripts." These scrolls were probably hidden there sometime during the second century B.C. by a Jewish group called the Essenes. They included fragments of every Old Testament Book in the Hebrew Bible with the exception of the Book of Esther.

Especially exciting was a complete scroll on the Book of Isaiah. The reason this discovery was so important was that until this event, the earliest copy we had of Isaiah's writings were made during the twelfth century A.D. Now scholars could move back over a thousand years closer to the time when the prophet actually wrote (around 700 B.C.). When a comparison was made between the Dead Sea copy and the twelfth century A.D. copy, they were both found to be almost identical, there once again reassuring us that our copy of God's Word today is indeed accurate and reliable!

B. The Greek Septuagint

The Greek Septuagint is a translation of the Old Testament Hebrew into the Greek language. This was done around 280 B.C. by the request of some Jewish leaders. The reason was because many Jews had moved into Egypt and other places outside of Palestine, and as a result, were unable to read or speak Hebrew. So, a translation was prepared in the common

Greek language of the day. It was called the "Septuagint" (the Greek word for seventy) because according to tradition it was supposedly translated by seventy Jewish scholars in seventy days. The Septuagint was the Bible in Jesus' day.

II. Publications up to the seventh century A.D.

A. The Papyri

This consisted of hundreds of sheets found in central Egypt in 1895. Some were stuffed in mummy cases and embalmed crocodile bodies. Among the various sheets was a 3½ x 2½-inch fragment containing John 18:31-38. Carbon-14 dating has shown this to have been written around 125 A.D. Thus this fragment is the oldest known Bible manuscript.

B. The Latin Vulgate

During the fourth century A.D. it was felt a new translation of the Bible was needed in Latin which was then the common language in the Western world. Thus, in 382 A.D. the great scholar Jerome was appointed by Damascus, the Bishop of Rome, to begin doing this. For the next twenty-five years Jerome worked on this, going right to the Hebrew and Greek. The term "vulgate" comes from the Latin word which means "common." Thus, until the King James Version in 1611, the Latin Vulgate became the recognized Bible for nearly 1200 years! In 1228 the Vulgate was divided into chapters by Stephen Langton, archbishop of Canterbury. It was divided into verses by Robert Stephens in 1551 and these verses were numbered by Montanus around 1571 A.D. The Vulgate was also the first Bible to be printed by John Gutenburg in 1455. One of these printed copies now resides in the U.S. Library of Congress and is valued at $350,000.

C. Codex Sinaiticus

This was an ancient manuscript of the Greek Septuagint, written approximately 330 A.D. It was discovered by the German Bible scholar Tischendorf in the monastery of St. Catherine on Mount Sinai in 1844. He noticed in a waste basket, waiting to be burned, vellum pages with Greek writings on them. The codex Sinaiticus contained 199 leaves of the Old Testament and the entire New Testament. On December 24, 1933 this codex which came so close to being burned was sold to the

British government by the Russians for $510,000, making it the most expensive book purchase of all time!

D. Codex Vaticanus

Also written around 330 A.D., it has been in the Vatican Library in Rome since 1481. Roman Catholic popes had constantly refused to allow competent Bible scholars to study it until the nineteenth century. It is thought that both this codex and the Mt. Sinai copy are two of the original fifty copies ordered by Emperor Constantine shortly after he assumed power over the Roman Empire in 312 A.D. It is however, incomplete, omitting the pastoral epistles, Philemon, Revelation, and the last few chapters of Hebrews.

E. Codex Alexandrinus

This is dated around 450 A.D. and was written in Egypt. In 1708 it was given to the Patriarch of Alexandria (where it got its name). In 1757 it was transferred to the British museum.

F. The Coptic Version

During the second century a new kind of language came into being which was sort of a cross between Greek and Egyptian. It became known as Coptic. Several translations were made at this time, around 350 A.D., of God's Word from the Greek into Coptic.

G. The Ethiopic Version

Ethiopia was the land south of Egypt in Africa. The Ethiopian eunuch of Acts 8:26-39 probably introduced Christianity there. This translation was a good verbal rendering of the Greek. It was fluent, readable, and helpful, and dates at around 350 A.D.

H. The Gothic Version

The land of the Goths was located north of the Danube River and west of the Black Sea. The Goths were an extremely warlike people. During one of their raids in Asia Minor they captured a young man named Ulfilos. Ulfilos was a Christian and a scholar who later translated the Scriptures into Gothic—with the exception of 1 and 2 Samuel and 1 and 2 Kings. The reason for this was due to the many wars recorded in these four Old Testament books. Ulfilos did not want to encourage the Goths along this line. The Gothic Version dated about 350

A.D., thus became the first translation of the Bible into a barbarian language! One of Ulfilos' versions still exists. It is called the Codex Argentus, and was written in gold and silver letters upon purple vellum. It now resides in the University Library at Upsala, Sweden.

I. The Armenian Version

Armenia is north of Mesopotamia. About 406 A.D. a great missionary and writer named Mesrob began translating into Armenian after reducing their language to a writing alphabet. The Armenian Version has been called "the most beautiful and accurate of all ancient versions—the Queen of Versions."

III. Publications in English from the Seventh Century to the Present.

Historians have classified the English language into three main periods. These are:

A. Old English Period—from 450 to 1100 A.D.

B. Middle English Period—from 1100 to 1500 A.D.

C. Modern English Period—from 1500 to date.

Keeping this outline in mind we shall now consider some major attempts to publish the Bible in English.

A. Old English Period—450 to 1100 A.D. There were at least ten known translators of the Bible during this period. The list would include a servant, two bishops, two monks, a king, two priests, an archbishop, and a hermit. Of these ten, we will examine the following three:

1. Caedmon (died in 680)

This stable worker at a monastery in North England did not translate the Bible on paper but rather memorized great portions of it and sang it with his harp in short lines of beautiful Celtic-Saxon verse wherever he traveled. He sang the story of Genesis, Exodus, a part of Daniel, the doctrines of the resurrection, ascension and the second coming of Christ, and that of heaven and hell.

2. Bede (674-735)

This godly monk, scholar, historian, and theologian is

often called today by the title of "the Father of English History." In his textbook, *General Biblical Introduction,* author H. S. Miller writes the following about Bede:

> His important work is the translation of the Gospel of John, which he finished just as he was breathing his last. All the day before Ascension Day, 735, the good old monk . . . had been dictating his translations, for he said, "I do not want my boys to read a lie, or to work to no purpose after I am gone."
>
> The next day he was very weak, and suffered much. His scribe said, "Dear master, there is yet one chapter to do, but it seems very hard for you to speak." Bede replied, "Nay, it is easy, take up thy pen and write quickly." In blinding tears the scribe wrote on. "And now father, there is just one sentence more." Bede dictated it and said, "write quickly." The scribe said, "It is finished, master." "Ay, it is finished!" echoed the dying saint, and with the Gloria chant upon his lips he passed to the great Master whom he had loved and served so long.[11]

3. Alfred (King of England, 871-901)
   Here Miller writes:
   > Alfred loved . . . the Bible. He was King, lawgiver, teacher, writer, translator. His wish was "that all the freeborn youth of his kingdom should employ themselves on nothing till they could first read well the English scriptures." He translated the ten commandments and other Old Testament laws, placing them at the head of his laws for England. He also translated the Psalms and the Gospels . . .[12]

B. Middle English Period—1100 to 1500 A.D. Here we will examine but one name—that of John Wycliffe!

John Wycliffe (1320-1384) has often been called "The Morning Star of Reformation." He was a great Oxford University teacher, preacher, reformer, and translator. Wycliffe was the first man to completely translate the entire Bible into the English language. By placing God's Word in the common language he thus did for England what Martin Luther would later do for Germany. His was the only English Bible for 145 years. As a sample of his English, note the following translation of the Lord's prayer:

> Our Fadir that art in hevenes, halewid be thi name; Thi king-

dom comme to, Be thi wille done in heven so in erthe; Gyve to us this dai oure breed over other substance, and forgive to us oure dettis as we forgyven to oure detouris; and leede us not into tempacioun, but delyvere us fro yvel.

C. Modern English Period—1500 to date

1. Tyndale's Version (1525)

If Wycliffe was known as the "Morning Star of Reformation," then Tyndale could rightly be called "The Milky Way of the Modern Bible." No other single man in history perhaps did as much in translating the Word of God for the people of God as did William Tyndale. Tyndale worked in constant danger, for under Catholic Emperor Charles V, it was a crime punishable by horrible torture, burning at the stake, or actual burial alive for anyone to read, purchase, or possess any New Testament book. But prior to his martyrdom, it is estimated that some 50,000 copies of the New Testament were circulated by this fearless and faithful servant of God. Early in 1526, Tyndale's New Testaments began pouring into England concealed in cases of merchandise, barrels, bales of cloths, sacks of flour and corn, and every other secret way which could be found. For every one the devil burned, God would allow Tyndale to publish three more to take its place!

It is thought that Tyndale's New Testament was based on the printed Greek New Testament text of the great scholar Erasmus (first printed on March 1, 1516), and that his Old Testament text was taken in part from the 1488 Hebrew publication. He also consulted the Latin Vulgate and Martin Luther's translation.

2. *The Coverdale Version* (1535 A.D.)

Miles Coverdale was born in 1488. He was converted to Christ and developed a strong love for the Scripture. He was a friend of Tyndale and later finished his Old Testament translation and revised his New Testament. It was a secondary translation; that is, it was based on previous translations of the Bible into Latin, German, and English. The reason for this is that Coverdale was not familiar with the Greek or Hebrew. The first edition came off the press on October 4, 1535. This was indeed a milestone for God's Word, as it marked the first whole Bible printed in English!

3. *Matthew's Version* (1537)

This version was prepared by John Rogers who used the pseudonym Thomas Matthew. The reason for this was that Rogers, known friend of Tyndale, felt his work would be more acceptable to various authorities if this relationship was not known. Rogers would later be burned to death during the reign of Bloody Mary in 1555. Matthew's Version was the first revision of the Tyndale Bible. It was approved by King Henry the VIII, who had hated Tyndale and his work. A divine irony is seen here.

4. *The Great Bible Version* (1539)

The notes and prefaces of Tyndale's and Coverdale's translations aroused so much argument that Henry VIII authorized a new version which would include no controversial footnote material. It was called the Great Bible because of its size. Due to its extreme value it was usually chained to a "reading post" within a church. In 1538 the King issued an injunction to all churches to purchase a copy of the Great Bible. This was to be paid for by the parson and parishoners. The importance of the Great Bible is that it became the first official English Bible "appointed to be read in all the churches." The King James Bible is basically a revision of the Great Bible.

5. *The Geneva Version* (1557)

During the vicious Protestant persecution under Bloody Mary, many reformers fled to Geneva, Switzerland, and enjoyed the protection of Geneva's great leader, John Calvin. It was here that Calvin's brother-in-law, William Whittingham, translated the Scriptures into the Geneva Version. This Bible became important for the following reasons:

a. It was the first version to divide the text into verses.
b. It was the first to omit the Apocrypha.
c. It was kissed by Queen Elizabeth (daughter of Henry VIII) at her coronation, a policy which is still followed by English kings and queens.
d. It was the most-loved Bible of the common people up to that time and went through more than 160 editions.
e. It was the Bible of Shakespeare and John Bunyan.
f. It was the Bible the pilgrims brought with them on the Mayflower in 1620 to America.

The text of the Geneva Bible was based on that of the Great Bible.

6. *The Bishop's Bible* (1568)

This version was translated because of the following reasons:

a. The Church of England did not like the notes in the Geneva Version.
b. The Geneva Version was undermining the authority of the Great Bible and that of the bishops.

It was translated by Matthew Parker, archbishop of Canterbury, aided by nine other bishops, thus its name, the Bishop's Bible. The Bishop's Bible was the second "Authorized Version" of the church, but was never accepted by the common people. In fact, Queen Elizabeth simply ignored it. The Bishop's Bible has gone down in history as the most unsatisfactory and useless of all the old translations.

7. *The Rheims—Douai Bible* (1582)

This version was an attempt by the Pope to win England back to the Roman fold, but he utterly failed. It was headed by William Allen and Gregory Martin, two Protestant turncoats from Oxford University. The name comes from the two places where the Old Testament and New Testament were produced. The Douai Version was therefore the first Catholic English Bible and was taken almost literally from the Latin Vulgate. The footnotes in this version strongly attacked all Protestant "heresies," and defended all Roman Catholic doctrine and practices.

8. *The King James Version* (1611)

One of the first tasks which King James I faced upon mounting his throne at the beginning of the seventeenth century was the reconciliation of various religious parties within his kingdom. The King James Version began with a request by Puritan spokesman Dr. Reynolds of Oxford concerning the feasibility of a new Bible translation. James agreed almost at once. He had disliked the popular Geneva Bible because of its footnotes. He also realized that neither the Geneva, nor the Great, nor the Bishop's version could be held up by him as a rallying point for Christians.

The following quote is from H. S. Miller—

> On July 22, 1604, the King announced that he had appointed 54 men as translators. The only indispensable qualification was that they should have proven efficiency as Biblical scholars . . . A list of 47 revisers has been preserved; the other seven may have died or resigned before the work had really begun.
>
> The revisers were organized into six groups, two meeting at Westminster, two at Cambridge, two at Oxford. One group at Westminster had Genesis to 2 Kings, the other had Romans to Jude: one group at Cambridge had 1 Chronicles to Ecclesiastes, the other had the Apocrypha; one group at Oxford had Isaiah to Malachi, the other had Matthew to Acts and Revelation. These men were the great Hebrew and Greek scholars of this day.
>
> Each reviser first made his own translation, then passed it on to be reviewed by each member of his group; then when each group had completed a book, a copy of it was sent to each of the other five groups for their independent criticism. Thus each book went through the hands of the entire body of revisers. Then the entire version, thus amended, came before a select committee of six, two from each of the three companies, and they ironed out ultimate differences of opinion, put the finishing touches . . . and prepared it for the printer.
>
> The revisers were governed by 15 rules, the gist of a few of them being: (1) The Bishop's Bible shall be followed and as little altered as the truth of the original will permit; (2) The old ecclesiastical words shall be retained; (3) The chapter divisions shall not be changed, unless very necessary; (4) No marginal notes at all, except explanation of Hebrew and Greek words which cannot be briefly and fitly expressed in the text; (5) Whenever the Tyndale, Matthew, Coverdale, the Great Bible, or the Geneva agrees better with the text than the Bishop's Bible, they are to be used.[13]

The King James Version also doubtless made usage of the four available printed Hebrew Old Testament Bibles at that time, and Erasmos' fifth edition of the Greek New Testament.

The King James Version is remarkable for many reasons. It was, first of all, undoubtedly the most beautiful, beloved, and popular translation of all time. It was also probably the only translation in which no parties involved had an axe to grind. In other words, it was a national undertaking in which no one had any interest at heart save that of producing the best possible version of the Scriptures!

It must be said however, that the King James Version was not immediately accepted by the general public. The Roman Catholics claimed it favored Protestantism. The Arminians said it leaned toward Calvinism. The Puritans disliked certain words like "bishop," "ordain," and "Easter." But after some forty years it overtook the popular Geneva Bible and has retained its tremendous lead ever since!

9. *The English* (1881-1885) and *American* (1901) *Revision*
By the latter part of the nineteenth century, the Church of England felt a new revision of the King James Version was needed for the following reasons:

a. The change in the meaning of some of the English words.
b. The discovery of new manuscripts since 1611.
c. The improved science of biblical criticism.
d. A better knowledge of the Greek and Hebrew.

Thus, on May 3, 1870 the initial formalities began. The Canterbury Convocation adopted five resolutions.

a. "We do not contemplate any new translation of the Bible, or any alteration of the language, except when in the judgment of the most competent scholars such change is necessary."
b. It offered a uniformity of renderings—that is, it translated the same Hebrew and Greek word by the same English word. The King James Version did not do this, but used a great variety of English words to translate a single Greek word. (For example, the Greek word *meno,* which means "to remain," is translated by ten different words in the King James Version. The Greek word *dunamis,* meaning "power," is translated by thirteen different English words.)
c. It translated the Greek tenses more accurately, especially the aorist and the imperfect tenses.
d. It translated the Greek definite article more accurately.
e. It translated the Greek preposition more accurately.

The English revised New Testament was published in England on May 17, 1881, and sale in the United States began on May 20. The excitement in this country about receiving a new version of the Bible was at an unbelievable high. For example, the people of Chicago wanted the New Testament about the same time New York would have it, and they could not wait until a fast train could bring it, so two Chicago dailies (the *Tribune* and the *Times*) had the first six books (Matthew to Romans, about 118,000 words) telegraphed from New York to Chicago (978 miles), by far the largest message ever sent over the wire! These papers then published all this on May 22, 1881.

But to the great disappointment of its friends, the English Version of 1881-1885 whose popularity had risen so high so fast almost immediately cooled off. People soon realized how much they would miss the familiar and loved words, phrases, grace, ease, poetry, and rhythm of the King James Version.

In 1901 the American Standard Version was published. This version offered several changes and improvements over its English cousin:

a. the substitution of "demon" for "devil," where the Greek read *daimon.*
b. the uniform rendering of "Holy Spirit" for "Holy Ghost."
c. the use of "who" instead of "which" in reference to persons. The King James Version phrase "Our Father, which art in heaven," became "Our father, who art in heaven."

Although the American Standard Version enjoyed better permanent reception than the English one, it still has not seriously cut into the lead of the King James Version.

10. *The Revised Standard Version* (1952)

This work has been one of the most controversial versions of the Bible ever published. The Revised Standard Version was authorized by the National Council of Churches of Christ in the U.S.A. and is the "official" version of this group. Hebrew scholar Dr. Merrill F. Unger sumarizes the Revised Standard Version in the following way:

Although this version has many excellencies, it is weak and

obscure in its translation of certain key Old Testament messianic passages.[14]

11. *The Amplified Bible* (1954)
This is a literal translation with multiple expressions using associated words to convey the original thought. The New Testament uses the Greek text of Westcott and Hort plus twenty-seven translations and revisions. The Old Testament is similarly extensive. The version is intended to supplement other translations authentically, concisely, and in convenient form.

12. *Good News for Modern Man* (1966)
This translation of the New Testament by Dr. Robert G. Bratcher (plus a distinguished review committee), is a paraphrase which gained enormous popularity in a short period of time. It was intended to communicate the Scriptures to the masses of English-speaking people around the world and has been much used as an instrument of evangelism for persons outside the church. It has since become available as a complete Bible called the Good News Bible.

13. *The Jerusalem Bible* (1966)
This is a translation from the Hebrew Masoretic, Greek Septuagint, Dead Sea Scrolls, and accepted Greek and Aramaic New Testament texts—all compared with the French Version. It was produced by twenty-eight principal collaborators in translation and literary revision under Alexander Jones, general editor.

14. *The New American Bible* (1970)
This is a Catholic translation that is a highlight of Bible publishing in the present century. All basic texts were consulted, and the work was twenty-six years in the making. Over fifty recognized biblical scholars, the majority of them college professors, labored to produce this outstanding version. Scholars were Catholic, Protestant, and Jewish. The purpose was to produce a more accurate translation from the older manuscripts, and this was made possible by the Pope in 1943. Prior to this version, Catholics had been required to use the later Vulgate as the basis for translation.

15. *The Living Bible* (1971)

An extremely popular paraphrase, (complete Bible 1971), this is the work of a single translator, Kenneth L. Taylor. The initial source was the American Standard Version of 1901, but Dr. Taylor and the Greek and Hebrew specialists he consulted for accuracy also used the most respected texts available.

16. *The New American Standard Bible* (1971)

This Bible was translated by an editorial board of fifty-four Greek and Hebrew scholars and required nearly eleven years to complete.

17. Other Major Versions Since 1950

The Holy Bible from Ancient Eastern Manuscripts (1957) has as its purposes to convey ancient biblical customs preserved only in the Aramaic texts and to reveal the deeper biblical meanings often hidden in idioms and parables.

The Berkeley Version in Modern English (1959) translates every word using modern terms.

The New English Bible (complete Bible 1970) required twenty-four years to complete and enlisted the labors of fifty recognized biblical scholars. It is based on the original Greek and Hebrew texts.

J. B. Phillips, an English vicar, has translated the New Testament into modern speech beginning with *Letters to Young Churches* (1947), followed by *The Gospels* (1952), *The Young Church in Action* (1955), the *Book of Revelation* (1957), and in 1958 the one-volume edition of his completed translation of the New Testament, *The New Testament in Modern Speech. Four Prophets* appeared in 1963.

PART EIGHT

Proofs that the Bible is the Word of God

Often the unbeliever hurls the following accusation at the believer: "Oh, you Christians—you're all alike! You're *so* dogmatic! You think you alone are right and everybody else is dead wrong! How can you possibly be so sure what you believe is true?" This question, even though often asked in a scoffing manner, is nevertheless a fair one. How *does* the child of God know his faith is the only correct one?

Let us suppose you are invited to an important social function in your home town. Attending this gathering are people from all over the world. As the introductions are being made, it slowly dawns on you that the only professing Christian there is yourself. You are subsequently introduced to a Buddhist, a Confucianist, a Shintoist, a Moslem, and other individuals, all belonging to various non-Christian religions. After a pleasant dinner, the conversation gradually turns to matters of religion. Your hostess, realizing this subject to be of general interest, suddenly announces:

> I have a wonderful idea! Since everyone here seems to have a great interest in religion, may I suggest we share with one another by doing the following: Each person will be allowed to speak uninterrupted for ten minutes on the subject, "Why I feel my faith is the right one."

The group quickly agrees with this unique and provocative idea. Then, with no warning, she suddenly turns to you and exclaims, "You go first!" All talk immediately ceases. Every eye is fixed on you. Every ear is tuned to pick up your first words. What, pray tell, would you say? How would you start? Let us quickly list a few arguments which you could *not* use.

1. You *couldn't* say, "I know I'm right because I *feel* I'm right! Christ lives in my heart!"

This of course *is* a wonderful truth experienced by all believers, but it would not convince the Buddhist who would doubtless feel Buddha lived in *his* heart!

2. You *couldn't* say, "I know I'm right because Christianity has more followers in this world than any other religion."

This is simply not true today. Actually, the sad truth is that evangelical, Bible-believing Christianity is a distinct minority in the world today. The Moslem would doubtless quickly point this out to you.

3. You *couldn't* say, "I know I'm right because Christianity is the oldest of all religions.

Ultimately, of course, this is true. But the Confucianist might contend that Confucius presented his teachings centuries before the Bethlehem scene. Of course, he would not understand the eternal existence of our Lord Jesus Christ.

These then are arguments you could not use. What then *could* you say? In reality you would have at your disposal only one single argument. But that argument, that weapon, used in the right way, would be more than enough to overwhelmingly convince any honest and sincere listener at a social gathering. That wonderful weapon, that unanswerable argument is one's own personal copy of the Bible! What could you say? Well, you could hold up your Bible and confidently proclaim the following:

> Look at this! I know I'm right because the author of my faith has given me a Book which is completely unlike any of the books of your faiths.

You could then continue (until your time runs out) by pointing out the unity, the indestructibility, and the universal influence of the Bible. You could discuss its historical, scientific, and prophetical accuracy. Finally, you might relate exciting examples of perhaps the greatest single proof of the supernaturalness of the Bible, and that is its marvelous, life-transforming power!

Of course it must be pointed out that neither the Word of God nor the God of the Word can be scientifically analyzed in a laboratory test tube. The divine Creator still desires and demands faith on the part of His creation. (See Heb. 11:1-6) But He has presented us with a heavenly textbook to aid us in this needed faith. In fact, the Gospel of John was specifically written—

> . . . that ye might believe that Jesus is the Christ, the Son of God; and that believing ye might have life through His Name (John 20: 31).

During the final phase of this study we will but briefly touch upon each of these "supernatural signs of the Scriptures," all of which indicate our Bible did in fact come from the very hand of

God! As the Christian acquaints himself with these amazing arguments, he is then qualified to:

> . . . sanctify the Lord God in your hearts: and be ready always to give an answer to every man that asketh you a reason of the hope that is in you . . . (1 Pet. 3:15).

I. First Supernatural Element—Its amazing unity!

That the Bible is a unity is a fact no honest reader can deny. In the preface of most Bibles, the thirty-nine Old Testament and twenty-seven New Testament books are listed in two parallel columns down the page. But a more accurate way would be to place the entire sixty-six collection in a clock-like circle, with Genesis occupying the first minute past twelve, Exodus the second, Leviticus the third, and so on. Finally, the book of Revelation would be placed on the number twelve, right next to Genesis! It is simply thrilling how these two books, Genesis the first and Revelation the last, perfectly dovetail together in a unity only God could create. For example:

In Genesis we read: "In the beginning God created the heaven and the earth" (1:1).
In Revelation we read: "I saw a new heaven and a new earth" (21:1).

In Genesis we see described the first Adam with his wife Eve in the Garden of Eden, reigning over the earth (1:27-28).
In Revelation we see described the last Adam with His wife, the Church, in the City of God, reigning over all the universe (21:9).

In Genesis we are told: "and the gathering of the waters called the seas" (1:10).
In Revelation we are told: "and there was no more sea" (21:1).

In Genesis God created the Sun and Moon, the day and the night (1:5, 16).
In Revelation "there shall be no night there" (22:5). "And the City had no need of the sun, neither of the moon, to shine in it: for the glory of God did lighten it, and the Lamb is the light thereof" (21:23).

In Genesis the Tree of Life is denied to sinful man (3:22).
In Revelation the Tree of Life "yielded her fruit every month: and the leaves of the tree were for the healing of the nations" (22:2).

In Genesis man hears God say: "Cursed is the ground for thy sake" (3:17).
In Revelation man will hear God say: "and there shall be no more curse" (22:3).

In Genesis Satan appears to torment man (3:1).
In Revelation Satan disappears, himself to be tormented forever (20:10)!

In Genesis the old earth was punished through a flood (7:12).
In Revelation the new earth shall be purified through a fire (2 Pet. 3:6-12; Rev. 21:1).

In Genesis, man's early home was beside a river (2:10).
In Revelation, man's eternal home will be beside a river—"and he shewed me a pure river of water of life, clear as crystal, proceeding out of the throne of God and of the Lamb (22:1).

In Genesis the patriarch Abraham weeps for Sarah (23:2).
In Revelation the children of Abraham will have God Himself wipe away all tears from their eyes (21:4).

In Genesis God destroys an earthly city, wicked Sodom, from the sands (Chapter 19).
In Revelation God presents a heavenly city, new Jerusalem, from the skies (21:1).

Genesis ends with a believer in Egypt, lying in a coffin (50:1-3).
Revelation ends with all believers in eternity, reigning forever (21: 4)!

A. This unity is achieved in spite of the long period of time involved in its writing.

1. More than fifteen centuries elapsed between the writing of Genesis and Revelation.

2. Nearly 400 years elapsed between the writing of Malachi and Matthew.

B. This unity is achieved in spite of the many authors (some forty) and their various occupations (approximately nineteen).

The Lord gave the Word: great was the company of those who published it (Ps. 68:11).

1. Moses was an Egyptian prince.
2. Joshua was a soldier.
3. Samuel was a priest.
4. David was a king.
5. Esther was a queen.
6. Ruth was a housewife.
7. Job was a rich farmer.
8. Amos was a poor farmer.

9. Ezra was a scribe.
10. Isaiah was a prophet.
11. Daniel was a prime minister.
12. Nehemiah was a cupbearer.
13. Matthew was a tax collector.
14. Mark was an evangelist.
15. Luke was a physician.
16. John was a wealthy fisherman.
17. Peter was a poor fisherman.
18. Jude and James were (?) carpenters.
19. Paul was a tentmaker.

C. This unity is achieved in spite of the different geographical places where the Bible was written.

1. In the desert (Exodus 17)
2. On Mt. Sinai (Exodus 20)
3. In Palestine (Most)
4. In Egypt (Jeremiah?)
5. On the Isle of Patmos (Revelation)
6. In Babylon (Daniel)
7. In Persia (Esther)
8. In Corinth (First and Second Thessalonians)
9. In Ephesus (Galatians ?)
10. In Caesarea (Luke ?)
11. From Rome (Second Timothy)

D. This unity is achieved in spite of the many different styles of its writing.

1. As history
2. As prophecy
3. As biography
4. As autobiography
5. As poetry
6. As law
7. In letter form
8. In symbolic form
9. In proverb form
10. In doctrinal form

Let us imagine a religious novel of sixty-six chapters which was begun by a single writer around the sixth century A.D. After the author had completed but five chapters, he suddenly dies. But during the next 1000 years, up to the sixteenth century, around 30 amateur "free lance" writers felt constrained to contribute to this unfinished religious novel. Few of these authors shared anything in common. Some of them were black, others white, still others yellow, and a few brown. They spoke different languages, lived at different times, in different countries, had totally different backgrounds and occupations, and wrote in different styles.

Let us furthermore imagine that at the completion of the thirty-ninth chapter the writing for some reason suddenly stops. Not one word is therefore added from the sixteenth until the twentieth century. After this long delay it begins once again by 8 new authors who add the final 27 chapters.

With all this in mind, what would be the chances of this religious novel becoming a moral, scientific, prophetic, and historical unity? The answer is obvious—not one in a million! And yet this is the story of the Bible!

II. Second Supernatural Element—Its Indestructibility!

The story is told of a visitor who toured a blacksmith shop. Viewing heaps of discarded hammers but only one huge anvil, he asked: "How often do you replace your anvil?" With a smile the owner replied, "Never! It is the anvil that wears out the hammers, you know!"

So it is with the Word of God! The hammers of presecution, ridicule, higher criticism, liberalism, and atheism have for centuries pounded out their vicious blows upon the divine anvil, but all to no avail. There they lay, in rusting piles, while the mighty anvil of the Scriptures stands unbroken, unshaken, and unchipped!

A. Its indestructibility in spite of political persecutions (from the Roman Emperors)

In 303 A.D., Emperor Diocletian thought he had destroyed every hated Bible. After many tireless years of ruthless slaughter and destruction, he erected a column of victory over the embers of a burned Bible. The title on the column read: "Extinct is the Name of Christian." Twenty years later, the new Emperor Constantine offered a reward for any remaining Bibles. Within 24 hours no less than fifty copies were brought out of hiding and presented to the king.

B. Its indestructibility in spite of religious persecutions

1. As seen through the persecutions by Roman Catholic popes.

Almost without exceptions, the early popes opposed the reading and translating of the Bible. In 1199, Pope Innocent III ordered the burning of all Bibles.

2. As seen through the persecutions leveled against John Wycliffe and William Tyndale.

Of all the heroes in church history no two other names are so closely associated with the Word of God than the names of Wycliffe and Tyndale. The very mention of these two men was no doubt sufficient to turn the devil livid with rage. It is therefore no surprise to read of the vicious attacks leveled against them.

a. John Wycliffe

Wycliffe lived at a time (the early part of the fourteenth century) when the burning question was: Who shall rule England, the king or the pope? Wycliffe believed the best way to break the grievous yoke of Romanism would be to place the Bible into the hands of the common people. This he did by translating (for the first time in history) the complete Bible into English. He then organized and sent forth a group of preachers (called the Lollards) to teach the Word of God all across England.

On December 28, 1384, while conducting a service in the Lutterworth Church, he was suddenly stricken with paralysis and died three days later. After his death, those who hated his Bible translation activities said the following things about Wycliffe:

> John Wycliffe, the organ of the devil, the enemy of the Church, the confusion of the common people, the idol of heretics, the looking glass of hypocrites, the encourager of schism, the sower of hatred, the storehouse of lies, the sink of flattery, was suddenly struck by the judgment of God . . . that mouth which was to speak huge things against God and against His Saints or holy church, was miserably drawn aside . . . showing plainly that the curse which God had thundered forth against Cain who also inflicted upon him. [From the mouth of a Monk]

> That pestilent wretch, John Wycliffe, the son of the old

> serpent, the forerunner of Antichrist, who had completed his iniquity by inverting a new translation of the Scriptures.[15]

One would almost conclude the Saviour had this in mind when He spoke the following words:

> These things have I spoken unto you, that ye should not be offended. They shall put you out of the synagogues: yea, the time cometh, that whosoever killeth you will think that he doeth God service. And these things will they do unto you, because they have not known the Father, nor me (John 16:1-3).

One final quotation from Miller's book seems appropriate here:

> In 1415, the Council of Constance which consigned John Hus and Jerome of Prague to a cruel death, demanded that the bones of the notorious heretic Wycliffe . . . be taken out of the consecrated ground and scattered at a distance from the sepulchre. Thirteen years later (1428), 44 years after his death, Pope Clement VIII, ordered no further delay; the grave was torn up, the coffin and skeleton borne down to the bank of the River Swift, a fire was kindled, the bones were burned, and the ashes thrown into the river. In the words of Thomas Fuller, so often quoted: "The Swift conveyed them into the Avon, the Avon into the Severn, the Severn into the narrow seas; they into the main ocean; and thus the ashes of Wycliffe are the emblem of his doctrine, which is now dispersed all the world over." [16]

b. William Tyndale (1484-1536)

Tyndale was one of the greatest translators of God's Word who ever lived. He was born in England, and so skilled in seven languages (Hebrew, Greek, Latin, Italian, Spanish, English, and Dutch), that whichever he might be speaking one would believe that language was his native tongue. Our own King James Version is practically a fifth revision of Tyndale's, and it retains many of the words and much of the character, form, and style of his version. In 1525, he printed the first copy ever produced of the New Testament in English. His overall goal in life was perhaps best expressed through a statement he made in 1521:

> I defy the Pope and all his laws; if God spares my life, ere many years I will cause a boy that driveth the plough shall know . . . the Scripture.[17]

In 1529, an amusing and thrilling event happened in England and Europe concerning the Word of God. Tyndale had been driven from England and had fled to Germany, but had continued producing New Testaments and slipping them back into England. One day, the Bishop of London (Bishop Tunstall), remarked to a British merchant, a man named Packington and a secret friend of Tyndale, of his desire to buy up all copies of the New Testament.

Said Packington, "My Lord, if it be your pleasure, I can buy them, for I know where they are sold, if it be in your Lord's pleasure to pay for them. I will then assure you to have every book of them that is imprinted."

Said the Bishop, "Gentle master Packington, do your diligence and get them; and with all my heart I will pay for them whatsoever they cost you, for the books are erroneous . . . and I intend to destroy them all, and burn them at St. Paul's Cross."

Packington then came to Tyndale and said, "William, I know that thou art a poor man, and hast a heap of New Testaments and books by thee, by the which thou hast endangered thy friends and beggared thyself; and I have now gotten thee a merchant, which with ready money shall dispatch thee of all that thou hast, if you think it so profitable to thyself."

"Who is the merchant," asked Tyndale.

"The Bishop of London," answered Packington.

"Oh, that is because he will burn them."

"Yes, marry, but what of that? The Bishop will burn them anyhow, and it is best that you should have the money for enabling you to imprint others instead."

"I shall do this," said Tyndale, "for these two benefits shall come thereof: First, I shall get money to bring myself out of debt, and the whole world will cry out against the burning of God's Word; and Second, the overplus of the money that shall remain to me shall make me more studious to correct the said New Testament, and so newly to imprint the same once again, and I trust the second will be much better than ever was the first." So the bargain was made. The bishop had the books, Packington had the thanks, and Tyndale had the money. Later, a man named Constantine was being tried as a heretic, and the judge promised him favor if he would tell how Tyndale received so much help in printing so many Testaments.

He replied, "My Lord, I will tell you truly: It is the Bishop of London that hath helped, for he hath bestowed among us a great deal of money upon the New Testaments to burn them, and that hath been, and yet is, our chief help and comfort." [18]

Again, to quote from Miller's textbook:

> On Friday, October 6, 1536, Tyndale was executed. By the Emperor's laws, only Anabaptists were burned alive, so he escaped that fate. He was led out and permitted to engage in a few moments of prayer. With fervent zeal and a loud voice he cried 'Lord, open the King of England's eyes!' Then his feet were bound to the stake, the iron chain was fastened around his neck, with a hemp rope loosely tied in a noose, and fagots and straw were heaped around him. At a given signal the rope was tightened, and Tyndale was strangled to death. Then the torch was applied, and the body was quickly consumed.[19]

C. Its indestructibility in spite of philosophical persecution

Here several cases come to mind:

1. Voltaire

He once said, "Another century and there will be not a Bible on the earth." The century is gone, and the circulation of the Bible is one of the marvels of the age. After he died, his old printing press and the very house where he lived was purchased by the Geneva Bible Society and made a depot for Bibles!

On December 24, 1933, the British Government bought the valuable Codex Sinaiticus from the Russians for half a million dollars. On that same day, a first edition of Voltaire's work sold for eleven cents in Paris bookshops!

2. Thomas Paine

He once said, "I have gone through the Bible as a man

would go through a forest with an axe to fell trees. I have cut down tree after tree; here they lie. They will never grow again." Tom Paine thought he had demolished the Bible, but since he crawled into a drunkard's grave in 1809, the Bible has leaped forward as never before.

3. Joseph Stalin

This bloody butcher took over all of Russia at the death of Lenin in the late twenties. From this point on until his death in the fifties, Stalin instituted a "ban the Bible" purge from the U.S.S.R. such as had never been witnessed before. This miserable man literally attempted to wipe the Word of God and the God of the Word from the Russian minds. Did he succeed? A recent poll taken in Russia shows that today more people than ever believe in God and His Word!

III. Third Supernatural Element—Its Historical Accuracy!

Less than a century ago, the agnostic took great glee in sneeringly referring to the "hundreds of historical mistakes" in the Bible! But then came the science of archaeology and with each shovel full of dirt the sneers have become less visible, until today they scarcely can be seen. Only a bigot or an ignoramus would now deny the historical merits of the Bible. When one thinks of historical scholarship and the Bible, three brilliant scholars of giant intellect and achievement come to mind. These three are:

A. Sir William Ramsey

For many years Ramsey was professor of humanity at the University of Aberdeen, Scotland. He was, in his time, the world's most eminent authority on the geography and history of ancient Asia Minor (called Turkey today). In his zeal to study every available early document concerning that period and area, he undertook an intensive research of the New Testament book of Acts and also the Gospel of Luke. This study, however, was approached with much skepticism. At that time he penned the following description of the book of Acts: ". . . a highly imaginative and carefully colored account of primitive Christianity."

But after many years of intensive study, this scholar, who began an unbeliever, became a staunch defender of the Word of God. The absolute historical accuracy of Luke's writings, even in the most minute details, captured first his brain and then his heart! Ramsey authored many books, but one of his better known is entitled: *The Bearing of Recent Discovery on the Trustworthiness of the New Testament.* Ramsey's overall opinion of the Bible is perhaps best seen in the following quote:

> I take the view that Luke's history is unsurpassed in regard to its trustworthiness . . . you may press the words of Luke in a degree beyond any other historian's and they stand the keenest scrutiny and the hardest treatment.

B. William F. Albright

One of the greatest and most respected oriental scholars who ever lived was William F. Albright. The list of his earned doctorate degrees reminds one of the old "New Deal" alphabetical organizations. These degrees included the Ph.D., Litt.D., D.H.L., Th.D., LL.D., DR.Hon. Caus. Dr. Albright writes the following concerning the Bible and his historical findings:

> The reader may rest assured: nothing has been found to disturb a reasonable faith, and nothing has been discovered which can disprove a single theological doctrine . . . We no longer trouble ourselves with attempts to 'harmonize' religion and science, or to 'prove' the Bible. The Bible can stand for itself.[20]

C. Robert Dick Wilson

Probably the most qualified Old Testament linguist of all time was Robert Dick Wilson. His skill along this line staggers the imagination. Dr. Wilson was born in 1856 and took his undergraduate work at Princeton University, graduating in 1876. He then completed both the M.A. and the Ph.D. After this, two years was spent at the University of Berlin in further postgraduate studies. Wilson taught Old Testament courses at Western Theological Seminary in Pittsburgh and returned to Princeton where he received international fame as a Hebrew scholar without peer. He was perfectly at home in over forty ancient Semitic languages! Dr. Wilson writes the following about himself:

> If a man is called an expert, the first thing to be done is to establish the fact that he is such. One expert may be worth more than a million other witnesses that are not experts. Before a man has the right to speak about the history and the language . . . of the Old Testament, the Christian Church has

> the right to demand that a man should establish his ability to do so. For forty-five years continuously, since I left college, I have devoted myself to the one great study of the Old Testament, in all its languages, in all its archaeology, in all its translations, and as far as possible in everything bearing upon its text and history. I tell you this so that you may see why I can and do speak as an expert. I may add that the result of my forty-five years of study of the Bible has led me all the time to a firmer faith that in the Old Testament we have a true historical account of the history of the Israelite people; and I have a right to commend this to some of those bright men and women who think that they can laugh at the old-time Christian and believer in the Word of God . . . I have claimed to be an expert. Have I the right to do so? Well, when I was in the Seminary I used to read my New Testament in nine different languages. I learned my Hebrew by heart, so that I could recite it without the intermission of a syllable . . . as soon as I graduated from the Seminary, I became a teacher of Hebrew for a year and then I went to Germany. When I got to Heidelburg, I made a decision. I decided—and did it with prayer—to consecrate my life to the study of the Old Testament. I was twenty-five then; and I judged from the life of my ancestors that I should live to be seventy; so that I should have forty-five years to work. I divided the period into three parts. The first fifteen years I would devote to the study of the languages necessary. For the second fifteen I was going to devote myself to the study of the text of the Old Testament; and I reserved the last fifteen years for the work of writing the results of my previous studies and investigations, so as to give them to the world. And the Lord has enabled me to carry out that plan almost to a year.[21]

Thus did Robert Dick Wilson write. One of the stirring moments in the experience of his students occurred when, after a dissertation on the complete trustworthiness of Scripture, the renowned scholar said with tears:

> Young men, there are many mysteries in this life I do not pretend to understand, many things hard to explain. But I can tell you this morning with the fullest assurance that—
>
> "Jesus loves me, this I know
> For the Bible tells me so." [22]

Of course, it must be admitted that no human intellect, however brilliant or accomplished, is infallible. But this fact should be kept in mind—no three other men among the many, who have criticized and ridiculed the Bible, were probably even half as qualified to speak with the authority as possessed by Ramsey, Albright, and Wilson!

In his valuable little work, *Unger's Bible Handbook,* the author lists no less than 96 examples of God's Word being authenticated by archaeology.

Halley's Bible Handbook tops even this number, listing some 112 examples. A summary of both these lists would include the following, all given to prove the historical accuracy of the Bible.

1. The Garden of Eden (Gen. 2:8-14)

   Archaeology has long established that the lower Tigris-Euphrates Valley in Mesopotamia (where Eden was located) was the cradle of civilization.

2. The Fall of man (Gen. 3:1-24)

   Many non-Hebrew cultures record this event. It is found in the Babylonian tablet called the Temptation Seal, in the Assyrian Archives, referred to as the Adam and Eve Seal, and in the Egyptian Library of Amen-hotep III.

3. The longevity of early mankind (Gen. 5:1-32)

   The oldest known outline of world history is the Weld-Blumdell Prism, written around 2170 B.C. This outline includes a list of eight pre-flood rulers. The shortest reign was said to have been 18,600 years, while the longest covered a period of 43,200 years. Of course this was gross exaggeration, but the point is that the historical root for all this may be found in the Genesis account which does accurately state that Methuselah did indeed live to be 969 years of age. A common objection to this and other so-called legends would claim that early mankind simply invented myths of their ancestors doing those things which they wished they could have done. But the fallacy of this argument may be demonstrated by the fact that there is no ancient legend of a nation or tribe of flying men, in spite of the fact that all men everywhere have always longed to soar into the skies!

4. The universal flood (Gen. 6:1—9:29)

   There is so much evidence concerning the flood in Noah's day that one scarcely knows just where to start. It can be demonstrated that, without exception, every major human culture has a lengthy flood tradition! Especially is this true in the ancient Babylonian civilization, as seen by their Epic of Gilgamesh. If the author may be allowed a personal illustration here, I am acquainted with a New Tribes missionary named Rod Wallin. Some years ago Rod began his work among a primitive people in the highlands of New Guinea. He was the first white man ever to set foot in that area. Many years were spent learning their difficult language. He then discovered to his astonishment that these natives had a detailed flood tradition!

5. The Tower of Babel (Gen. 11:1-9)

   Over two dozen ancient temple towers in Mesopotamia called Ziggurats have been excavated.

6. Abraham's birthplace (Gen. 11:27-31)

   World famous archaeologist C. L. Wooley's excavation in 1922-34 in Mesopotamia has made Ur of the Chaldees one of the best-known ancient sites of all times. When Abraham left Ur in 2000 B.C. the city was at the height of its splendor as a commercial and religious center! (See also Joshua 24:2.)

7. Abraham's visit to Egypt (Gen. 12:10-20)

   Due to space problems, many of the following Old Testament events which have been authenticated by archaeology will simply be alluded to and not expanded upon.

8. Abraham's battle with the kings in Genesis 14.

9. The destruction of Sodom and Gomorrah (Gen. 18-19)

   William Albright found at the Southeast corner of the Dead Sea great quantities of relics of a period dating between 2500 and 2000 B.C., with evidence of a dense population which for some reason ceased abruptly around 2000 B.C. The evidence indicated an earthquake and an explosion.

10. Joseph and Potiphar's wife (Genesis 39)

    There is an Egyptian story entitled *A Tale of Two Brothers* which may have for its foundation the events related in Genesis 39.

11. The Seven-Year Famine (Gen. 41:46-57)

12. Israel's entrance into Egypt (Exod. 1:1-6)
13. The episode of the bricks without straw (Exod. 1:11; 5:7-19)
14. Moses' birth (Exod. 2:10)
15. The death of Pharaoh's first-born (Exod. 12:29)
16. The Exodus (Exod. 12:1-14:31)
17. The fact of Rahab's house located on Jericho's wall (Josh. 2:15)
18. The fall of Jericho (Josh. 6:1-27)

    The archaeologist Garstang found evidence that Jericho was destroyed about 1400 B.C., (about the date given to Joshua) and that the walls had fallen flat, outward, and down the hillside. This was extremely unusual, for had the city been captured the usual way, its walls would have been pushed inward by the ramming weapons of that day. He also found the layer of ashes left by Joshua's fire! (See Josh. 6:24.)
19. Deborah's victory of the Canaanites (Judges 4:23, 23; 5:19)
20. Saul's reign (1 Sam. 9:1–31:13)
21. David's conquests (2 Sam. 1:1–24:25)
22. Solomon's gold (1 Kings 14:25-26)
23. Solomon's stables (1 Kings 9:19; 10:26-29).

    The Oriental Institute has found the ruins of his stables with their stone hitching-poles and mangers.
24. Solomon's copper furnaces (1 Kings 7)
25. Solomon's navy (1 Kings 9)
26. Jeroboam's calves (1 Kings 12:25-33)
27. Shishak's invasion (1 Kings 14:25-28)
28. The building of Samaria by Omri (1 Kings 16:24)
29. The rebuilding of Jericho (1 Kings 16:34)

30. Ahab's house of ivory (1 Kings 22:39)
31. Jezebel's cosmetic box (2 Kings 9:30)
    The actual saucers in which she mixed her cosmetics have been found in Samaria among the ruins of Ahab's ivory house.
32. The Assyrian captivity of northern Israel (2 Kings 15: 29)
33. The tunnel of Hezekiah (2 Kings 20:20; 2 Chron. 32: 3-4)
34. Manasseh's reign (2 Kings 21:1-15)
35. Esther's palace (Esth. 1:2)
36. The Babylonian captivity of Judah (2 Kings 25)
37. The reign of Belshazzar (Dan. 5)
38. The fall of Babylon (Dan. 5)
39. The edict of Cyrus (Ezra 1:2-3; 2 Chron. 36:22-23)
40. The repentance of Nineveh in Jonah's day (Jonah 4)
    History has shown that during the reign of Shalmaneser II (the King of Nineveh in Jonah's time), there was a sudden religious movement which resulted in a change from the worship of many gods to that of one God whom they called Nebo. Nebo was probably the Assyrian name for the Hebrew *Elohim* (Gen. 1:1). It would seem that in earlier days he had been worshiped as the supreme and only God. To the worship of this God the nation now returned!

IV. Fourth Supernatural Element—Its Scientific Accuracy!

It has previously been discussed in this study that although the Bible is primarily a spiritual message from God and not a specific scientific textbook, all scientific statements found in the Scriptures must nevertheless be taken literally and at face value! The devoted believer will find little time for the claim that while we may look to God for the who and why of creation, we must depend upon the scientist for the how and when of this creation. Actually the Bible contains far more specific scientific statements than one might realize. Some of these precepts would include:

A. The fact that the earth is spherical

Some seven centuries B.C. the Hebrew prophet Isaiah wrote:

> It is he that sitteth upon the circle of the earth . . . (Isa. 40: 22).

While it is true that a few Greek philosophers did postulate this as early as 540 B.C., the common man held the earth to be flat until the introduction of the compass and the fifteenth-century voyages of Columbus and Magellan.

B. The fact that the earth is suspended in space

The book of Job is thought to be one of the oldest in the Bible, written perhaps earlier than 1500 B.C. At this time one of the most advanced "scientific" theories concerning the earth was that our planet was flat and rested securely upon the back of a gigantic turtle who was slowly plodding through a cosmic sea of some sort! But note the refreshing (and accurate) words of Job:

> He stretcheth out the north over the empty place, and hangeth the earth upon nothing (Job 26:7).

All this was not known by the scientists of the world until the writings of Sir Isaac Newton in 1687 A.D.

C. The fact that the stars are innumerable

Nearly twenty centuries B.C., God spoke to Abraham one night and said:

> Look now toward heaven, and tell the stars if thou be able to number them: and he said unto him. So shall thy seed be (Gen. 15:5).

Abraham must have at first wondered about this! God was promising him to be the founder of a nation whose descendants would be as uncountable as the stars! But Abraham could count the stars. There they were— a little under 1200 visible to the naked eye. Was his future nation to be limited to this number? Although we are not told so, he must have reasoned that perhaps there were "a few more" up there that he couldn't see! And he would not be disappointed, for today scientists tell us there are probably as many stars in the heavens as there are grains of sand on all the sea shores of the world! In fact, in a previous conversation with Abraham, God used this very comparison—

And I will make thy seed as the dust of the earth: so that if a man can number the dust of the earth, then shall thy seed also be numbered (Gen. 13:16).

Thus does the Bible describe the heavens. (See also Jer. 33:22; Heb. 11:12.) But what about the scientific opinion of that day?

As late as 150 A.D., the famous astronomer Ptolemy dogmatically declared the number of the stars to be exactly 1056!

D. The fact that there are mountains and canyons in the sea

As recently as a century or so ago, the ocean's volume and size was viewed as a watery bowl, which sloped from the coastline gently downward until the middle, where it was deepest. It then was thought to proceed upward to the other side. Of course we now know this to be totally untrue. Some of the highest mountains and deepest canyons are located on the floor of the Pacific Ocean! In fact, the deepest hole yet found is the Marianas Trench, just off the Philippines; it is over seven miles deep!

But long before ocean science discovered this, the Bible graphically described it. During one of his songs of deliverance, David spoke of the canyons of the sea (2 Sam. 22:16), and a backslidden prophet described the submerged mountains during the world's first submarine trip! (See Jonah 2:6).

E. The fact that there are springs and fountains in the sea

Shortly after World War II, research ships discovered many underwater volcanoes. The number is estimated today to be at least 10,000. Further research by Dr. William W. Rubey of the U.S. Geological Survey has shown the present rate of water increase from underwater volcanic outlets to be 430 million tons each year. The earth's heat drives the entrapped water from underground molten rock and forces it out through one of these natural openings.

This interesting fact is vividly described in at least three Old Testament passages. (See Gen. 7:11; 8:2; Prov. 8:28.)

F. The fact that there are watery paths (ocean currents) in the sea

In his booklet, *Has God Spoken?*, author A. O. Schnabel writes the following:

David said in Psalms 8:8 that God had subjected all things to men, including: "Whatsoever passeth through the path of the sea." The Hebrew word "paths" carries the literal meaning of "customary roads."

Matthew Fountaine Maury is called "The Pathfinder of the Seas." This American is the father of today's oceanography and responsible for the establishment of Annapolis Academy. A statue of Maury stands in Richmond, Virginia—charts of the sea in one hand, and Bible in the other. Until Maury's efforts there were no charts or sailing lanes. One day during a temporary illness, his eldest son was reading to him from the Bible, and read Psalms 8:8. Maury stopped him and said, "read that again." After hearing it again, he exclaimed, "It is enough—if the Word of God says there are paths in the sea, they must be there, and I am going to find them." Within a few years he had charted the sea lanes and currents. His *Physical Geography of the Sea* was the first textbook of modern oceanography.[23]

G. The fact of the hydrologic cycle

This would include precipitation, evaporation, cloud construction, movements of moisture by wind circuits, etc. (See Eccles. 1:6-7; Job 26:8; 36:27, 28; 38:25-27; 37:16; Ps. 135:7.)

H. The fact of the invisible atom structure of matter

The modern era of atomic physics did not begin until 1895 with the discovery of X-rays. Prior to this, men reasoned that all matter was built from visible things. But scientists now understand that all matter is held together by attraction and energy—things which are not apparent. With all this in mind, consider the following Scripture passages:

> Who being the brightness of his glory, and the express image of his person, and upholding all things by the word of his power, when he had by himself purged our sins, sat down on the right hand of Majesty on high (Heb. 1:3).
>
> Now faith is the substance of things hoped for, the evidence of things not seen (Heb. 11:1).
>
> And he is before all things, and by him all things consist (Col. 1:17).
>
> For the invisible things of him from the creation of the world are clearly seen, being understood by the things that are made,

> even his eternal power and Godhead; so that they are without excuse (Rom. 1:20).

I. The fact that all living things are reproduced after their own kind

> And God created great whales, and every living creature that moveth, which the waters brought forth abundantly, after their kind, and every winged fowl after his kind: and God saw that it was good (Gen. 1:21).

> And of every living thing of all flesh, two of every sort shalt thou bring into the ark, to keep them alive with thee; they shall be male and female (Gen. 6:19).

For hundreds of years scientists followed the spontaneous generation theory of Aristotle (350 B.C.). They believed eggs of all lower animals (insects, etc.) were formed out of rotting substance. Frogs and other small sea life had their origin in slime pools. In fact, it was not until 1862 that Louis Pasteur proved once for all that there was no such thing as spontaneous generation. Then, in 1865, a monk named Johann Mendel demonstrated even more forcibly the rigid laws of heredity. But one could learn all this in the first few chapters of the Bible!

J. The facts involved in health and sanitation

The great law given in the Bible was Moses', of course, who established hundreds of rules to govern health and sanitation. Moses grew up in the court of Pharaoh, spending the first forty years of his life there. About this time a famous ancient medical book called *The Papyrus Ebers* was being written in Egypt. Because of Egypt's role in the world at that time, this work soon achieved fame as the official standard for its day. Actually it was filled with quack cures, old wives' tales, and practically every false superstition of its day. In his book *None of These Diseases,* author S. McMillen writes:

> Several hundred remedies for diseases are advised in the Papyrus Ebers. The drugs include "lizard's blood, swine's teeth, putrid meat, stinking fat, moisture from pig's ears, milk goose grease, asses' hoofs, animal fats from various sources, excreta from animals, including human beings, donkeys, antelopes, dogs, cats, and even flies." [24]

The point of all the above is simply this—Moses was well acquainted with all the medical knowledge of his day. Yet in all his writings and proven remedies concerning health and sanitation, he never once even indirectly refers to the false "cures" found in the Papyrus Ebers! Let us now examine what he did prescribe for the health of marching Israel:

1. Concerning sickness

Moses gave comprehensive laws concerning sickness. These included laws for those having leprosy or cases with open sores. He thus laid down rules for the recognition of infected individuals, for quarantine or isolation, and concerning the uncleanness of anything touched by these people. In other words, Moses recorded laws comparable to modern health and sanitation practice in most civilized countries today. Again, to quote from *None of These Diseases:*

> For many hundreds of years the dreaded disease leprosy had killed countless millions of people in Europe. The extent of the horrible malady among Europeans is given by Dr. George Rosen, Columbia University professor of Public Health: "Leprosy cast the greatest blight that threw its shadow over the daily life of medieval humanity. Not even the Black Death in the fourteenth century . . . Produced a similar state of fright. . . ."
>
> What did the physicians offer to stop the ever-increasing ravages of leprosy? Some taught that it was brought on by eating hot food, pepper, garlic and the meat of diseased hogs. Other physicians said it was caused by malign conjunctions of the planets. Naturally, their suggestions for prevention were utterly worthless . . . what (finally) brought the major plagues of the Dark Ages under control? George Rosen gives us the answer: "Leadership was taken by the church, as the physicians had nothing to offer. The church took as its guiding principle the concept of contagion as embodied in the Old Testament . . . This idea and its practical consequences are defined with great clarity in the book of Leviticus . . . once the condition of leprosy had been established, the patient was to be segregated and excluded from the community. Following the precepts laid down in Leviticus the church undertook the task of combatting leprosy . . . it accomplished the first great feat . . . in methodical eradication of disease." [25]

2. Concerning sanitation

Two quotes from Dr. McMillen are helpful here:

> Up to the close of the eighteenth century, hygenic provisions, even in the great capitols, were quite primitive. It was the rule for excrement to be dumped into the streets which were unpaved and filthy. Powerful stenches gripped villages and cities. It was a heyday for flies as they bred in the filth and spread intestinal disease that killed millions.
>
> Such waste of human lives that could have been saved if people had only taken seriously God's provision for freeing man of diseases! With one sentence the Book of books pointed the way to deliverance from the deadly epidemics of typhoid, cholera, and dysentery: "You shall set off a place outside the camp and, when you go out to use it, you must carry a spade among your gear and dig a hole, have easement, and turn to cover the excrement" (Deut. 23:12-13, Berkeley).[26]

Dr. McMillen goes on to say that until the beginning of this century there was a frightful mortality rate in the hospitals of the world due to infection caused by the lack of doctors washing their hands! In the maternity ward alone of the world famous Vienna Medical Center Hospital one out of every six women died due to infection. McMillen then writes:

> Such mortality would not have occurred if surgeons had only followed the method God gave to Moses regarding the meticulous method of hand washing and changing of clothes after contact with infectious diseases . . . the Scriptural method specified not merely washing in a basin, but repeated washings in running water, with time intervals allowed for drying and exposure to sun to kill bacteria not washed off.[27]

3. Concerning circumcision

Some final thoughts from McMillen are extremely appropriate here. In the third chapter of his book he discusses the astonishing scarcity of cervical cancer among Jewish women. Medical science has now attributed this blessing to the rite of circumcision practiced by Jewish males. This simple operation prevents the growth of cancer-producing Smegma bacillus which during physical relations can be transferred from the uncircumcised male to the female. McMillen then writes:

> There is one final but remarkably unique fact about the matter of circumcision. In November, 1946, an article in

> *The Journal of the American Medical Association* listed the reasons why circumcision of the newborn male is advisable. Three months later a letter from another specialist appeared in the same journal. He agreed heartily with the writer of the article on the advantages of circumcision, but he criticized him for failing to mention the safest time to perform the operation. This is a point well taken. L. Emmett Holt and Rustin McIntosh report that a newborn infant has a peculiar susceptibility to bleeding between the second and fifth days of life . . . It is felt that the tendency to hemorrhage is due to the fact that the important blood-clotting element, Vitamin K, is not formed until the fifth to the seventh day . . . a second element which is also necessary for the normal clotting of blood is prothrombin . . . It appears (based on data from the science of Pediatrics) that an eight-day old baby has more available Prothrombin than on any other day in its entire life. Thus one observes that from a consideration of Vitamin K and prothrombin determinations the perfect day to perform a circumcision is the eighth day.[28]

Keeping all this in mind, one simply marvels at the accuracy of the Book when the following passage is read:

> And God said unto Abraham, Thou shalt keep my covenant therefore, thou, and thy seed after thee in their generation. This is my covenant, which ye shall keep between me and you and thy seed after thee; Every man child among you shall be circumcised. And ye shall circumcise the flesh of your foreskin; and it shall be a token of the covenant betwixt me and you. And he that is eight days old shall be circumcised among you, every man child in your generations, he that is born in the house, or bought with money of any stranger, which is not of thy seed (Gen. 17:9-12).

K. The facts involved concerning the human bloodstream

The Bible is, among other matters, an expert on human blood! In Lev. 17:11, God lays down one of His key statements concerning this subject. Here He declares:

For the life of the flesh is in the blood.

One searches in vain to read in this ancient Book any reference whatsoever to that false medical practice known as bloodletting which plagued mankind from the fourth century B.C. until the nineteenth century A.D. Only eternity will reveal how many sick individuals were actually killed through this "cure." No other non-biblical writer understood the nature of the blood. In fact, many scientists (Herophilos for example, a physician in the medical museum at Alexandria, Egypt), believed blood to be a carrier of *disease* instead of life. The death of our own George Washington is thought to have been due in part to excessive bloodletting!

L. The facts involved in the two laws of thermodynamics

Apart from gravity itself, two of the most solid and immutable laws in all physics are the first and second laws of thermodynamics. Albert Einstein himself testified that in all the known universe there is no time nor place where the two do not apply.

1. The First Law of Thermodynamics—that of energy conservation.

This law states that although energy can change forms, it cannot be either created or destroyed and therefore the sum total remains constant. Thus no energy is now being created or destroyed anywhere in the known universe.

2. The Second Law of Thermodynamics—that of energy deterioration.

This law states that when energy is being transformed from one state to another, some of it is turned into heat energy which cannot be converted back into useful forms. In other words this universe may be looked upon as a woundup clock that is slowly running down.

These two absolute laws were not fully realized nor established by scientists until around 1850 A.D. Yet there are literally dozens of specific references to these laws in the Word of God.

1. Passages describing the First Law—

> Thus the heavens and the earth were finished, and all the host of them. And on the seventh day God ended his work which he had made; and he rested on the seventh day from all his work which he had made. And God blessed the seventh day, and sanctified it: because that in it he had rested from all his work which God created and made (Gen. 2:1-3).

> By the word of the Lord were the heavens made; and all the host of them by the breath of his mouth. He gathered the

> waters of the sea together as an heap: He layeth up the depth in storehouses. Let all the earth fear the Lord: let all the inhabitants of the world stand in awe of him. For he spake, and it was done; he commanded, and it stood fast (Ps. 33:6-9).

> Of old hast thou laid the foundation of the earth: and the heavens are the work of thy hand (Ps. 102:25).

> For we which have believed do enter into rest, as he said, As I have sworn in my wrath, if they shall enter into my rest: although the works were finished from the foundation of the world. . . . For he that is entered into his rest, he also hath ceased from his own works, as God did from his (Heb. 4: 3, 10).

2. Passages describing the Second Law—

> They shall perish, but thou shalt endure: yea, all of them shall wax old like a garment: as a vesture shalt thou change them, and they shall be changed (Ps. 102:26).

> For I reckon that the sufferings of this present time are not worthy to be compared with the glory which shall be revealed in us. For the earnest expectation of the creature waiteth for the manifestation of the sons of God. For the creature was made subject to vanity, not willingly, but by reason of him who hath subjected the same in hope. Because the creature itself also shall be delivered from the bondage of corruption into the glorious liberty of the children of God. For we know that the whole creation groaneth and travaileth in pain together until now. And not only they, but ourselves also, which have the firstfruits of the Spirit, even we ourselves groan within ourselves, waiting for the adoption, to wit, the redemption of our body (Rom. 8:18-23).

> And, Thou, Lord, in the beginning hast laid the foundation of the earth; and the heavens are the works of thine hands: They shall perish; but thou remainest; and they all shall wax old as doth a garment; And as a vesture shalt thou fold them up, and they shall be changed: but thou art the same, and thy years shall not fail (Heb. 1:10-12).

It may be furthermore stated that God brought the First Law into being after the original creation (see Gen. 1:31) and instituted the Second Law after man's fall (Gen. 3:17). Finally, it may be said that both laws will be rescinded after the Great White Judgment.

> For, behold, I create new heavens and a new earth: and the former shall not be remembered, nor come into mind (Isa. 65:17).

> For as the new heavens and the new earth, which I will make, shall remain before me, saith the Lord, so shall your seed and your name remain (Isa. 66:22).

> Nevertheless we, according to his promise, look for new heavens and a new earth, wherein dwelleth righteousness (2 Pet. 3:13).

> And I saw a new heaven and a new earth: for the first heaven and the first earth were passed away; and there was no more sea. And I John saw the holy city, new Jerusalem, coming down from God out of heaven, prepared as a bride adorned for her husband. And I heard a great voice out of heaven saying, Behold, the tabernacle of God is with men, and he will dwell with them, and they shall be his people, and God himself shall be with them, and be their God. And God shall wipe away all tears from their eyes; and there shall be no more death, neither sorrow, nor crying, neither shall there be any more pain: for the former things are passed away. And he that sat upon the throne said, Behold, I make all things new. And he said unto me, Write: for these words are true and faithful (Rev. 21:1-5).

Here then are at least twelve scientific principles accurately described in the Bible, some of them centuries before man discovered them. Not only does the Word of God include that which is scientifically correct, but it also totally avoids the scientific nonsense that is found in all other ancient religious writings.

The Egyptians believed the world was hatched from a great cosmic egg. The egg had wings and flew. This resulted in mitosis.

They also believed the sun was a reflection of earth's light, and that man sprang from little white worms they found in the slime and ooze after the overflow of the Nile. In the sacred Vedas of India we read:

> The moon is 50,000 leagues higher than the sun, and shines by its own light; night is caused by the sun's setting behind a huge

> mountain, several thousand feet high, located in the center of the earth; that this world, flat and triangular is composed of seven states—one of honey, another of sugar, a third of butter, and still another of wine, and the whole mass is borne on the heads of countless elephants which in shaking produce earthquakes.

In the Library of the Louvre in Paris there are three and a half miles of obsolete science books. In 1861 the French Academy of Science published a brochure of fifty-one "scientific facts" which supposedly contradicted the Bible. These were used by the atheists of that day in ridiculing Christians. Today all fifty-one of those "facts" are UNacceptable to modern scientists.

Surely the devout Christian can utter a hearty amen with Dr. James Dwight Dana of Yale University, probably the most eminent geologist in American history, who once addressed a graduating class in these words:

> Young men! As you go out into the world to face scientific problems, remember that I, an old man who has known only science all his life long, say to you, that there is nothing truer in all the Universe than the scientific statements contained in the Word of God!

V. Fifth Supernatural Element—Its Prophetical Accuracy!

One of the acid tests of any religion is its ability to predict the future. In this area (as in all other areas) the Bible reigns supreme. One searches in vain through the pages of other sacred writings to find even a single line of accurate prophecy. Some seven centuries B.C. the Hebrew prophet Isaiah wrote:

> Let them . . . shew us what shall happen . . . or declare us things for to come. Shew the things that are to come hereafter, that we may know that ye are gods . . . (Isa. 41:22-23).

So be it! We now consider the amazingly accurate prophecies under the following categories:

A. Prophecies dealing with the nation Israel

1. Israel would become a great nation—Gen. 12:1-3.
2. Her kings would come out of the tribes of Judah—Gen. 49:10.

3. She would spend 400 years in Egypt—Gen. 15:13.
4. The nation would suffer a civil war—1 Kings 11:31.
5. The nation would spend seventy years in Babylon—Jer. 25:11; 29:10.
6. She would return (in part) to Jerusalem after the seventy years—Dan. 9:1-2.
7. Israel would eventually be scattered among the nations of the world —Deut. 28:25, 64; Lev. 26:33.
8. Israel would become a byword among these nations—Deut. 28:37.
9. Israel would loan to many nations, but borrow from none—Deut. 28:12.
10. She would be hounded and persecuted—Deut. 28:65-67.
11. Israel would nevertheless retain her identity—Lev. 26:44; Jer. 46:28.
12. She would remain alone and aloof among the nations—Num. 23:9.
13. Israel would reject her Messiah—Isaiah 53.
14. Because of this, her enemies would dwell in her land—Lev. 26:32; Luke 21:24.
15. Jerusalem would be destroyed—Luke 19:41-44; 21:20.
16. Israel would, in spite of all these things, endure forever—Gen. 17:7; Isa. 66:22; Jer. 31:35-36; Matt. 24:34.
17. Israel would return to Palestine in the latter days prior to the Second Coming of Christ—Deut. 30:3; Ezek. 36:24; 37:1-14; 38:1—39:29.

B. Prophecies dealing with various nations.

1. Edom

Esau, Jacob's brother, was the founder of the nation Edom (see Genesis 36). Years after his death, Edom refused to help Israel, the nation founded by Jacob (see Numbers 20) and actually delighted in persecuting them. Because of this, God pronounced doom upon them. According to various biblical prophecies:

a. Their commerce was to cease.
b. Their race was to become extinct.
c. Their land was to be desolate. (See Jer. 49:17-18; Ezek. 35:3-7; Book of Obadiah; Mal. 1:4.)

All this has taken place in spite of her unbelievably strong fortified Capital, Petra. In 636 A.D. Petra was captured by Mohammed, and shortly after this Petra and Edom drop from the pages of history.

2. Babylon

Babylon was the first of four world powers mentioned in Dan. 2:31-43 and 7:1-8. Daniel prophesied the demise of mighty Babylon, as did Isaiah (13:17-19) and Jeremiah (51:11). This literally happened on the night of October 13, 539 B.C. when Darius the Median captured the city by diverting the course of the Euphrates River which had flowed under the walls of the city. (See Daniel 5.)

3. Media-Persia

One of the most remarkable passages on prophecy is found in Dan. 8:1-7,20,21, written beside a river in 551 B.C. In a vision Daniel is told of a series of battles that would not take place until some 217 years later. Here the prophet describes for us the crushing defeats of Darius III (here pictured as a ram) by the Greek Alexander the Great (symbolized as a he-goat). This took place in three decisive battles —Granicus, in 334 B.C.; Issus, in 333 B.C.; and Gaugamela, in 331 B.C.

4. Greece

In this same chapter, Daniel predicts the dissolution of the Greek empire upon the death of Alexander into four smaller and separate powers, each ruled over by one of his generals (Dan. 8:8, 20, 21; 7:6). This happened in exact detail in 301 B.C. after Alexander died of a raging fever at the age of thirty-three in Babylon.

5. Rome

In Dan. 2:40-41 we read:

> And the fourth kingdom shall be as strong as iron: forasmuch as iron breaketh all these, shall it break in pieces and bruise. And whereas thou sawest the feet and toes, part of potter's clay, and part of iron, the kingdom shall be divided . . .

Here Daniel rightly predicted that Rome, the fourth kingdom (which would come into power between the times of Nebuchadnezzar and Christ) should be "as strong as iron."

And so Rome was. By 300 B.C. Rome had become a major power in the Mediterranean world. By 200 B.C., she had conquered Carthage, her arch enemy. In 63 B.C., the Roman general Pompey entered Jerusalem. Daniel noted in his prophecy, however, that, "The kingdom shall be divided." This, of course, happened in 364 A.D.

6. Egypt

Some 600 years before Christ, the prophet Ezekiel wrote:

> . . . The word of the Lord came unto me, saying . . . set thy face against Pharaoh, King of Egypt, and prophecy against him, and against all Egypt. It shall be the basest of the kingdoms; neither shall it exalt itself any more above the nations: For I will diminish them, that they shall no more rule over the nations (Ezek. 29:1, 2, 15).

The history of Egypt is, of course, one of the oldest in recorded Western civilization. The country was united into a single kingdom about 3200 B.C. and was ruled by a succession of dynasties down to the time of Alexander the Great, who conquered Egypt in 332 B.C. We note that Ezekiel does not predict the disappearance of Egypt, as he did concerning Edom (35:3-7), but simply the demise of Egypt. The prophecy was that Egypt would be cut short and never again become a world power! This prophecy has been fulfilled to the last letter.

7. Russia

Ezekiel 38:39. (Russia will be treated under that section dealing with prophecies concerning last-day conditions.)

C. Prophecies dealing with specific cities

1. Tyre

Ezekiel's prophecy in chapter 26 concerning the city of Tyre is surely one of the greatest in the entire Bible. Tyre was actually two cities, one on the coastline, some sixty miles northwest from Jerusalem, and the other on an island, a half mile out in the Mediterranean Sea. In this prophecy, Ezekiel predicts:

a. The Babylonian king, Nebuchadnezzar, was to capture the city.
b. Other nations would later participate in Tyre's destruction.
c. The city was to be scrapped and made flat, like the top of a rock.
d. It was to become a place for the spreading of nets.
e. Its stones and timber were to be laid in the sea (Zech. 9:3-4).
f. The city was never to be rebuilt.

Has all this taken place? Consider the following historical facts:

a. Ezekiel wrote all this around 590 B.C. Some four years later, 586 B.C., Nebuchadnezzar surrounded the city of Tyre. The seige lasted thirteen years and in 573 B.C. the coastal city was destroyed. But he could not capture the island city. During the next 241 years the island city of Tyre dwelt in safety and would have doubtless ridiculed Ezekiel's prophecy concerning total destruction.

b. But in 332 B.C. Alexander the Great arrived upon the scene and the island city was doomed. Alexander built a bridge leading from the coastline to the island by throwing the debris of the old city into the water. In doing this he literally scrapped the coastline clean. (Some years ago an American archaeologist named Edward Robinson discovered forty or fifty marble columns beneath the water along the shores of ancient Tyre.)

After a seven-month seige, Alexander took the island city and destroyed it. From this point on, the surrounding coastal area has been used by local fishermen to spread and dry their nets.

c. Tyre has never been rebuilt in spite of the well-known nearby freshwater springs of Roselain, which yield some 10,000 gallons of water daily.

2. Jericho

In the sixth chapter of Joshua we see described the fall of Jericho's walls and the subsequent destruction of the city. Immediately after this, Joshua makes an amazing threefold prophecy about this fallen city. He stated:

a. that Jericho would be rebuilt again by one man.
b. that the builder's oldest son would die when the work on the city had begun.
c. that the builder's youngest son would die when the work was completed (see Josh. 6:26).

Joshua uttered those words around 1450 B.C. Did this happen? Some five centuries after this, in 930 B.C., we are told:

a. that a man named Hiel from Bethel rebuilt Jericho.
b. that as he laid the foundations, his oldest son, Abiram, died.
c. that when he completed the gates, his youngest son, Segub, died. (See 1 Kings 16:34.)

3. Nineveh (Nahum 1-3)

During the time of Jonah, God had spared the wicked city of Nineveh by using that Hebrew prophet (after an unpleasant submarine trip) to preach repentance. But the city had soon returned to its evil ways. So around 650 B.C., another prophet, Nahum, predicted the complete overthrow of Nineveh.

At the time of this prophecy, Nineveh appeared to be impregnable; her walls were one hundred feet high and broad enough for chariots to drive upon. The city had a circumference of sixty miles and was adorned by more than 1,200 strong towers.

In spite of all this, the city fell, less than forty years after Nahum's prophecy. An alliance of Medes and Babylonians broke through her walls during August of 612 B.C., after a two-month siege. The victory was due in part to the releasing of the city's water supply by traitors within. The destruction was so total that Alexander the Great marched his troops over the desolate ground which had once given support to her mighty buildings, and never knew there had once been a city there!

4. Jerusalem (Matt. 24:1-2; Luke 19:41-44; 21:20-24)

These sad words were uttered by Jesus Himself. He predicted Jerusalem would be destroyed, her citizens would be slaughtered, and her temple would be completely wrecked, with not one stone left upon another.

This all literally happened less than forty years later. In February of 70 A.D., the Roman general Titus surrounded Jerusalem with 80,000 men to crush a revolt that had begun some five years back. In April of that year he began the siege in earnest. Conditions soon became desperate within the city walls. Women ate their own children, and grown men fought to the death over a piece of bird's dung for food! Finally, in September of the same year, the walls were battered down and the slaughter began. When the smoke had cleared, over a half-million Jews lay dead. A number of these had been crucified by Titus. Eventually the temple was leveled and the ground under it plowed up, just as our Lord had predicted!

D. Prophecies dealing with particular individuals

1. Josiah

The following incident concerns a wicked Israelite king named Jeroboam:

> And, behold, there came a man of God out of Judah by the word of the Lord unto Bethel: and Jeroboam stood by the altar to burn incense. And he cried against the altar in the word of the Lord, and said, O altar, altar, thus saith the Lord; Behold a child shall be born unto the house of David, Josiah by name; and upon thee shall he offer the priests of the high places that burn incense upon thee, and men's bones shall be burnt upon thee (I Kings 13:1,2).

This all took place in 975 B.C. Some 350 years went by; the year was 624 B.C. We are told of the actions of a new king of Israel:

> Moreover the altar that was at Bethel and the high place which Jeroboam the son of Nebat, who made Israel to sin, had made, both that altar and the high place he broke down, and burned the high place, and stamped it small to powder, and burned the grove. And as Josiah turned himself, he spied the sepulchres that were there in the mount, and sent, and took the bones out of the sepulchres, and burned them upon the altar, and polluted it, according to the word of the Lord which the man of God proclaimed, who proclaimed these words (2 Kings 23:15,16).

2. Cyrus

Perhaps the greatest Old Testament prophet was Isaiah. For some sixty-two years this eloquent and godly man wrote and preached. But even though Jerusalem was at rest when he ministered, Isaiah predicted her captivity (as did also Jeremiah; see Jer. 25:12; 29:10) and subsequent restoration.

> That saith of Cyrus. He is my shepherd, and shall perform all my pleasure: even saying to Jerusalem, Thou shalt be built; and to the temple, Thy foundation shall be laid (Isa. 44:28).

Isaiah penned these words around 712 B.C. By 606 B.C., Nebuchadnezzar, the Babylonian king, had captured Jerusalem and had led many captive Jews (see Psalm 137) into his capital. For seventy long years they remained here. This was all predicted, of course, by Jeremiah (see Jer. 25:12; 29:10). Then, in 536 B.C., the miracle happened! The prophet Ezra tells us of this:

> . . . that the Word of the Lord . . . might be fulfilled, the Lord stirred up the spirit of Cyrus . . . that he made a proclamation throughout all his kingdom, and put it also in writing, saying, Thus saith Cyrus . . . The Lord God of heaven hath . . . charged me to build an house at Jerusalem, which is in Judah (Ezra 1:1-2).

So then, Isaiah rightly predicted that Cyrus would allow the Jews to return and rebuild their temple in Jerusalem 176 years before it happened!

3. Alexander the Great

Although Daniel does not refer to him by name, there seems little doubt that Alexander is the "he-goat" mentioned in Dan. 8:3-8.

Alexander was the first real world conqueror. He crossed the Hellespont in the spring of 334 B.C. and soon met and crushed the Persian troops at the battle of Issus in 333 B.C. Josephus, the Jewish historian, tells us that when Alexander approached Jerusalem, he was met at the gates by the high priest, who thereupon proceeded to show him that his victories over the Persians had all been prophesied by Daniel in 553, some 220 years in advance. The Greek warrior was reportedly so impressed at all this that he worshiped the high priest and spared Jerusalem!

4. Antiochus Epiphanes

Like Alexander, Antiochus is not mentioned by name, but is surely referred to in Dan. 8:9-14. Antiochus was a blood-thirsty, Jew-hating Syrian general who conquered Palestine in 167 B.C. He then entered the temple Holy of Holies and horribly desecrated it by slaughtering a hog on the altar! Here Daniel forsaw this terrible event some 386 years before it happened.

5. John the Baptist

In Isa. 40:3-5, the prophet correctly describes the future message of John the Baptist 700 years in advance. (See also Matt. 3:1-3.)

E. Prophecy of the Seventy Weeks

We now briefly consider the most important, the most amazing, and the most profound single prophecy in the entire Word of God! It was written by Daniel who was living in Babylon along with thousands of other Jewish captives. The year was around 550 B.C. Daniel had been reading Jeremiah's prophecy which said that after a seventy-year captivity period, God would permit the Jews to return to Jerusalem(see Jer. 25:11; 29:10). As Daniel studied those words, he began to pray, confessing his sins and the sins of Israel.

During this powerful and tearful prayer, the angel Gabriel appeared to Daniel and related to him the prophecy of the seventy weeks.

> Seventy weeks are determined upon thy people and upon thy holy city, to finish the transgression, and to make an end of sins, and to make reconciliation for iniquity, and to bring in everlasting righteousness, and to seal up the vision and prophecy, and to anoint the most holy. Know therefore and understand, that from the going forth of the commandment to restore and to build Jerusalem unto the Messiah the Prince shall be seven weeks, and threescore and two weeks: the street shall be built again, and the wall, even in troublous times. And after threescore and two weeks shall Messiah be cut off, but not for himself . . . (Dan. 9:24-26).

In his correspondence course on the book of Daniel, Dr. Alfred Martin of the Moody Bible Institute writes:

> The expression translated "seventy weeks" is literally "seventy

sevens." Apart from the context one would not know what the "sevens" were. One would have to inquire, "sevens of what?" This expression in Hebrew would be as ambiguous as if one were to say in English, "I went to the store and bought a dozen." A dozen of what? One of the basic principles of interpretation is that one must always interpret in the light of the context, that is, in the light of the passage in which a given statement occurs. As one searches this context, remembering that the vision was given in answer to the prayer, one notes that Daniel had been reading in Jeremiah that God would "accomplish seventy years in the desolations of Jerusalem" (Dan. 9:2). This is the clue. Daniel is told in effect: Yes, God will accomplish seventy years in the captivity; but now He is showing you that the whole history of the people of Israel will be consummated in a period of seventy sevens of years! [29]

In other words, God tells Daniel He would continue to deal with Israel for yet another 490 years before beginning in everlasting righteousness! Let us now examine this time period in some detail.

1. The 490-year period was to be divided into two sections. The first would cover 483 years (or, 69 weeks) and the second would span seven years (one week).

2. The 490-year time period was to begin at the rebuilding of Jerusalem's walls. The first two chapters of Nehemiah informs us that this occurred during the twentieth year of Artaxerxes' accession. The Encyclopedia Britannica sets this date on March 14, 445 B.C.

3. The brilliant British scholar and Bible student, Sir Robert Anderson, has reduced the first period of 483 years into its amount of days. This he has done by multiplying 360 (the days in a biblical year) by 483. The total number of days then in this first period is 173,880. He then suggests that if one begins counting on March 14, 445 B.C., and goes forward, that these days would run out on April 6, 32 A.D. It was on this very day that Jesus made His triumphal entry into the city of Jerusalem!

> And when he was come near, he beheld the city and wept over it, saying, If thou hadst known, even thou, at least in in this thy day, the things which belong to thy peace! But now they are hid from thine eyes (Luke 19:41-42).

Of course it was on this same day also that the Pharisees sought to kill Jesus (Luke 19:47). Thus, Daniel, some five and one half centuries before, correctly predicted right down to the very day the tragic passion week of our Lord, resulting with the cutting off of Israel's Messiah!

F. Prophecies dealing with last-day conditions

An old weather proverb says, "Red at night is the sailor's delight; red in the morning is the sailor's warning." Of course we are specifically told that neither man nor angel can know the exact time when Christ shall come again (Mark 13:32-33). But are we to be given any signs or indications that the last days are upon us? We are indeed. Our Lord Himself said: ". . . when ye shall see all these things, know ye that it is near, even at the doors" (Matt. 24:33). What things?

Keeping in mind our weather proverb, it may be said that there are at least eleven "red signs" in the sky of prophecy!

1. The increase of wars and rumors of war

On the headquarters of the United Nations in New York there is inscribed the words of Micah 4:3:

> . . . and they shall beat their swords into plowshares, and their spears into pruninghooks: nation shall not lift up a sword against nation, neither shall they learn war any more.

This of course will be literally realized some glorious day, but not until the Prince of Peace comes to reign on this earth! Until that day, both Daniel (Dan. 9:26) and Jesus (Matt. 24:6) warned of continual war. It has been pointed out by the Society of International Law at London that there have been only 268 years of peace during the last 4,000 years of human history, despite the signing of more than 8,000 separate peace treaties!

In February of 1914, a prophecy conference was held in Los Angeles, sponsored by Bible-believing people. When the sessions were completed, a liberal religious magazine entitled *The Christian Advocate* sneeringly dubbed this prophecy conference a "pathetic conference," because the conference held the Bible taught wars would continue and intensify until the advent of Christ.

But the sneers soon disappeared, for in August of that very year, the guns of World War I commenced their deadly thunder, and they continue belching their missiles of destruction to this day!

Until the coming of Christ, the U.N. would have more correctly inscribed the fearful words of Joel 3:9-10:

> Proclaim ye this among the Gentiles; Prepare war, wake up the mighty men, let all the men of war draw near; let them come up: Beat your plowshares into swords, and your pruning hooks into spears.

2. Extreme Materialism

Materialism has been defined as "that science of knowing the price of everything, and the value of nothing." Paul warned of this:

> This know also, that in the last days perilous times shall come. For men shall be lovers of their own selves, covetous, boasters, proud, blasphemers, disobedient to parents, unthankful, unholy (2 Timothy 3:1,2).

This seemed to be the thrust of our Lord's message to His disciples in Luke 17:26-30. In this passage He told them that similar conditions which prevailed in the days of Noah and Lot (prior to the flood and the destruction of Sodom) would prevail in the last days. He went on to describe how they ate, drank, married, bought, sold, planted, and built. They lived and died as if there was no divine judge or coming judgment. God and grace had been replaced by gold and graft!

In Rev. 3:14-19, the apostle John warns that this soul-murdering materialism would also worm its way into the local church. Here we read God's chilling indictment of the Laodicean church:

> I know thy works, that thou art neither cold nor hot: I would thou wert cold or hot. So then because thou art lukewarm, and neither cold nor hot, I will spue thee out of my mouth. Because thou sayest, I am rich, and increased with goods, and have need of nothing; and knowest not that thou art wretched, and miserable, and poor, and blind, and naked.

3. Lawlessness

This word perhaps more closely describes our world today than any other single word in the English language. In 2 Tim. 3:2-4 we are told:

> For men shall be lovers of their own selves, covetous, boasters, proud, blasphemers, disobedient to parents, unthankful, unholy, without natural affection, trucebreakers, false accusers, incontinent, fierce, despisers of those that are good, traitors, heady, highminded, lovers of pleasures more than lovers of God.

And so men are! How appropriate the words of the psalmist:

> . . . a stubborn and rebellious generation; a generation that set not their heart aright, and whose spirit was not stedfast with God (Ps. 78:8).

This spirit of lawlessness is seen in every aspect of our civilization today. Men blow their noses on their country's flags and wipe their feet on its constitutions, all the while plotting to murder their own law officers!

To help man live an orderly life down here, God originally formed three divine institutions, that of marriage (Genesis 2, Ephesians 5), human government (Genesis 9, Romans 13), and the church (Matthew 16). These three institutions are held in open contempt by millions today.

This spirit of rebellion has spread from the home to the streets, and recently manifested itself in military life (that last stronghold of discipline), where certain types of soldiers now feel free to murder unpopular officers by mangling their bodies with hand grenades! The apostle Jude reminded us of all this when he wrote:

> But beloved, remember ye the words which were spoken before of the apostles of our Lord Jesus Christ; How that they told you there should be mockers in the last time, who should walk after their own ungodly lusts. These be they who separate themselves, sensual, having not the Spirit (Jude 1:17-19).

(See also Eph. 2:2; Rom. 1:30; Prov. 17:11; Psalm 2.)

4. Overpopulation

Dr. Henry Morris has written:

> A remarkable commentary on human history is the fact that man as a whole has broken all God's comandments except the very first. Immediately after the creation of man, God said to him: "Be fruitful and multiply and fill the earth" (Gen. 1:28).[30]

Because of this, the earth was filled with mankind at the time of the Flood (Gen. 6:1). Dr. Morris goes on in his book to demonstrate through some impressive population ratio equations the probability of humanity increasing in the 1656 years from Adam to Noah from the original two people to over three billion individuals! In a recent and highly popular book, Dr. Paul Ehrlich of Stanford University writes:

> It has been estimated that the human population of 6000 B.C. was about five million people . . . The population did not reach 500 million until almost 8000 years later—about 1650 A.D. This means it doubled roughly once every thousand years or so. It reached a billion people around 1850 then doubling in some 200 years. It took only 80 years or so for the next doubling, as the population reached two billion around 1930. We have not completed the next doubling to four billion yet, but we now have well over three billion people. The doubling time at present seems to be about 37 years. Quite a reduction in doubling times: 1000 years, 200 years, 80 years, 37 years.[31]

These statements become especially significant in the light of Jesus' statement that similar conditions would prevail in the last days as prevailed in the days of Noah! (See Luke 17:26-27.)

5. An increase in speed and knowledge

At the end of a long and faithful ministry, the aged prophet Daniel is instructed to write down the following words of God:

> But thou, O Daniel, shut up the words, and seal the book, even to the time of the end: many shall run to and fro, and knowledge shall be increased (Daniel 12:4).

After reading this passage many years ago, the great scientist-Christian Sir Isaac Newton is reported to have said:

> Personally I cannot help but believe that these words refer to the end of times. Men will travel from country to country in an unprecedented manner. There may be some inventions which will enable people to travel much more quickly than they do now.

This was written around 1680 A.D. Newton went on to speculate that this speed might actually exceed 50 m.p.h.

Some eighty years later, the famous French atheist, Voltaire, read Newton's words and retorted:

> See what a fool Christianity makes of an otherwise brilliant man! Here a scientist like Newton actually writes that men may travel at the rate of 30 or 40 m.p.h. Has he forgotten that if man would travel at this rate he would be suffocated? His heart would stand still! [32]

One wonders what Voltaire would have said had he known that some two centuries after he wrote this, an American astronaut, Edward H. White, on June 3, 1965, would climb out of a spacecraft a hundred miles high and casually walk across the continental United States in less than fifteen minutes, strolling along at 17,500 m.p.h.? We wonder indeed! Or that during the recent moon landings, man exceeded a speed some twelve times faster than a 22-caliber rifle bullet travels?

In this same prophecy, Daniel predicts an intensification of knowledge. Our country is still less than two hundred years old. Yet, during this time we have developed the public educational system from absolutely nothing to its present fantastic level. We now have over 60 million students in America alone, attending some 72,000 public elementary schools, 27,000 secondary schools, and 1200 college and universities! Each year we spend $36 billion to finance all this!

6. A departure from the Christian faith:

This sign is, no doubt, both the most evident and the most tragic of all. We are specifically warned of this in at least four New Testament passages:

> Let no man deceive you by any means: for that day shall not come, except there come a falling away first . . . (2 Thess. 2:3).

> Now the Spirit speaketh expressly, that in the latter times some shall depart from the faith . . . (1 Tim. 4:1).

> For the time will come when they will not endure sound doctrine; but after their own lusts shall they heap to themselves teachers, having itching ears; And they shall turn away their ears from the truth, and shall be turned unto fables (2 Tim. 4:3-4).

> Knowing this first, that there shall come in the last days scoffers, walking after their own lusts, and saying, Where is the promise of his coming? For since the fathers fell asleep, all things continue as they were from the beginning of the creation (2 Peter 3:3-4).

In a recent editorial, a leading Chicago newspaper puzzled over the fact that some of the most vicious attacks on the Bible of late have come not from the Communists or atheists, but from the throats and pens of professing Christian theologians! With all his hatred for God, Adolf Hitler never once hinted that the Creator of the universe might be dead! No, the "God is dead" twaddle came from a religion professor!

The National Council of Churches is perhaps the worst offender. While there are doubtless sincere men within the NCC, the thrust and bulk of the movement is decidedly anti-Bible. In the past, this group has preferred communism to democracy, encouraged immorality, supported anarchy, downplayed every important Christian doctrine, ridiculed Bible believers, and weakened the faith of millions. Paul's sad prediction has been fulfilled down to the last letter when he wrote:

> Having a form of godliness, but denying the power thereof . . . (2 Tim. 3:5).

7. Intense demonic activity

In 1 Tim. 4:1-3, Paul warns—

> Now the Spirit speaketh expressly, that in the latter times some shall depart from the faith, giving heed to seducing spirits, and doctrines of devils; Speaking lies in hypocrisy; having their conscience seared with a hot iron; forbidding to marry, and commanding to abstain from meats . . .

During the earthly ministry of Jesus there was a great outburst of demon activity (of His thirty-six recorded miracles, seven were performed to cast out demons), and according to Paul, we may expect the same hellish activity just prior to our Lord's second coming. Demonic influence is behind many popular movements. At least five immediately come to mind, the first two being mentioned by Paul in the above passage of Scripture.

a. Forbidding to marry

Demons have always attempted to break up homes, but in the last days an attempt will be made to destroy the very institution of marriage itself! The present woman's liberation movement certainly lends itself to this unholy attempt, as does the infamous W.I.T.C.H. group (Woman's International Terrorist Conspiracy from Hell). The major premise of these and similar groups is this—that marriage is Victorian, unnecessary, and degrading to the modern twentieth-century liberated female! Of course the advocates of all this also support free love, the homosexual "gay" movement, and loudly demand the immediate repeal of all abortion laws.

b. Commanding to abstain from meats

One of the truly phenomenal developments during the sixties in America was the tremendous impact of eastern religious creeds upon our society. Zen Buddhism is flourishing among our young people. Soka Gakkai, originally a Japanese religion, now claims 170,000 U.S. members. Since the Beatles made their pilgrimage to India, Eastern attitudes can be heard in many acid-hard rock and roll songs. This has all been brought out to say that the oriental mind is often vegetarian in practice and pantheistic in thought.

c. The usage of hard drugs

The mind and body-destroying drug problem in our country can be summarized in two words—uncontrollable and unsolvable. The total weight of confiscated illegal drugs in America during 1969 was over 35 tons! In New York there are over 100,000 heroin addicts alone. The pushers of poison are now distributing their foul merchandise within the confines of many grade schools. Unless this menace is soon checked, LSD may well command more influence than the PTA in our lower educational systems!

d. The revival of astrology

Astrology is a pseudoscience which attempts to determine the influence of stars upon the lives of people. Recent archaeological findings indicate the original purpose of the ancient Tower of Babel (see Genesis 11) was to provide an elevated platform for this very thing. God hated it then as He does today. Astrology is rapidly becoming a multi-billion dollar racket in the United States. Untold thousands of otherwise sane individuals will not buy, sell, travel, or any number of other things without carefully checking the order of the stars!

c. The revival of witches and mediums

One of the saddest commentaries on apostate Protestantism was witnessed in the tragic life of the late Episcopalian bishop James Pike. Pike's drug-tormented son had killed himself and Pike, like Saul of old, decided to consult his own witch of Endor to speak with his dead son.

Books on witchcraft now abound and some colleges offer courses on the art of the black magics. In many homes the words of Jean Dixon carry far more weight than those of Jesus Christ!

8. The unification of the systems of this world

According to Rev. 13:4-8,16,17 the Antichrist will someday successfully unite the religious, political, and economic systems of the earth under his evil control. Although this goal will not be fully achieved until he assumes complete power, we can nevertheless see the approaching stormclouds.

9. In the religious field

In the past few years we have witnessed several world-wide efforts for religious unity. For example:

(1) Protestants are uniting with Protestants

In 1968, the United Methodist Church was formed in Dallas by the union of the Methodist Church and the Evangelical United Brethren Church. In 1961, the United Church of Christ came into being by the union of the Evangelical and Reformed Church, and the Congregational Christian Church. Many other successful united efforts could be mentioned among Lutherans, Presbyterians, and other Protestant groups.

(2) Protestants are uniting with Roman Catholics.

On June 19, 1969, in Switzerland, a historic photo was taken which showed Pope Paul VI and Eugene Carson

Blake, secretary general of the World Council of Churches, both bowed in prayer in the Geneva Ecumenical Center.

(3) The World Council of Churches is uniting with various heathen religions. This is true in spirit, if not by letter. In 1955, to celebrate the tenth anniversary of the United Nations, a special "Festival of Faith" was held in the San Francisco Cow Palace. This was reported in *The National Council Outlook,* official organ of the National Council of Churches. Here we read:

> Today, in the United Nations mankind finds new hope for the achievement of Peace. This hope was given dramatic expression last June 19 when some 16,000 persons of every race, creed, and color assembled in San Francisco's Cow Palace to pray for peace and pledge their support to the United Nations . . .
>
> There were Christians and Jews, Buddhists and Confucianists, Hindus and Moslems—men whose names are household words around the world, and workaday folk.
>
> They called God by different names—speaking to Him in different tongues, but the dream for peace in their hearts was the same—and the prayers on their lips echoed the prayers of people around the world. Initiated by the San Francisco Council of Churches, the Festival of Faith was a symbol for all men of the oneness of their aspirations . . .
>
> High point of the prayer meeting was the recitation together of the Responsive Reading composed of sentences from the sacred books of the six faiths represented—Christian, Jewish, Moslem, Buddhist, Hindu, and Confucian.[32]

b. In the political world

In 1942, the United Nations Pact was signed in Washington D.C. by twenty-six nations. Today there are some 126 nations and countries belonging to the U.N. However, one may in general place these 126 nations into three basic categories: (1) the United States and her allies, (2) Russia and her allies, and (3) the Neutrals, who attempt to milk the best from the first two! The Bible indicates that during the first half of the Tribulation, political world power will be concentrated in three main areas: the West (probably America and Western Europe), the North (Russia and Eastern Europe), and the East (perhaps China and India?) Thus even now we see the outlines of these future political power blocks!

c. In the economic world

In 1854 Commodore Matthew Perry, a U.S. naval officer, forced the opening of Japanese trade with the West. In the 118 years that have followed, the economic dependence and cooperation of not only the East and West, but of all the world's nations has been no less than amazing! No major country escaped the terrible depression of the thirties. It has been rightly claimed that, economically speaking, when Chicago sneezes, the entire world shivers!

9. Recent developments in Russia (Ezekiel 38 and 39)

Some years back, Dr. Joshua Kunitz, a professor at London University, wrote a book about Russia and titled it, *Russia, the Giant that Came Last*. No better words could have been chosen to describe the U.S.S.R. The rise of Russia has been nothing less than phenomenal! Even though her land began to be peopled by the Slavs as early as the fifth century A.D., Russia remained a geographical void for the next thousand years. Then came Peter the Great and the world began to take notice. In 1712 he transferred the capital from Moscow to St. Petersburg. After this, Catherine the Great appeared on the scene (1762-1796) with her attempts to westernize Russia. Russia's place in world history was now assured. But how clumsy she was in those days! She was soundly defeated by tiny Japan in 1905. In 1914 she entered World War I, only to suffer crushing defeat. In October of 1917 the Communist Lenin took over all of Russia with some 40,000 followers. The statistics of growth of communism from this point on are beyond comparison—from 40,000 in 1917 to more than one billion today. This amounts to an increase of more than two million percent! God-hating and Christ-rejecting communism continues in Russia today as it did during that black October.

Some 2,600 years ago, the Hebrew prophet Ezekiel prophecied that such a nation would rise to the north of Palestine just prior to the second coming of Christ. He writes of this in chapters 38 and 39.

a. The name of this land would be Rosh (see Ezek. 38:2 in the American Standard Version). He continues by mentioning two cities of Rosh. These he called Mesheck and Tubal (38:2). The names here are remarkably similar to Moscow and Tobolsk, the two ruling capitals of Russia today!

b. This land would be anti-God, and therefore God would be against it (Ezek. 38:3).

c. Russia (Rosh) would invade Israel in the latter days (38:8).

d. This invasion would be aided by various allies of Rosh (38:5-6), such as: Iran (Persia), South Africa (Ethiopia), North Africa (Libya), Eastern Europe (Gomer), and the Cossacks of southern Russia (Togarmah). In 38:15 Ezekiel describes the major part horses will play during this invasion. The Cossacks of course have always owned and bred the largest and finest herd of horses in history!

e. The purpose of this invasion was "to take a spoil" (38:12). If one but removes the first two letters from this word *spoil,* he soon realizes what Russia will really be after!

This, then, is Ezekiel's prophecy concerning Russia. Of course there are many who would criticize all this, and accuse Bible believers of simply waiting to see what happens and then twisting current events into their own peculiar prophetical scheme. To answer this, the following quotes are given. It will be observed by the dates that both statements were written long before Russia became the power she is today!

> Russia is evidently destined to become the master of Asia. Her frontier line across Asia will be 5000 miles in length. We believe, from the place assigned to Russia in the Word of God, that her legions will sweep over the plains and mountains of Asia and will become the dominant power over all the East (Walter Scott, *The Prophetical News and Israel's Watch,* June, 1888).

> This king of the North I conceive to be . . . Russia. Russia occupies a momentous place in the prophetic word (John Cumming in 1864).

10. Recent developments in Palestine

Shortly before His crucifixion, our Lord uttered the following words:

> Now learn a parable of the fig tree; When his branch is yet tender, and putteth forth leaves, ye know that summer is nigh; So likewise ye, when ye shall see all these things, know that it is near, even at the doors. Verily I say unto you, This generation shall not pass, till all these things be fulfilled (Matt. 24:32-34).

Jesus spoke this to answer His disciples' question as to when He would come again. He told them to "learn a parable of the fig tree." In the Gospels, the fig tree is almost always a symbol for the nation Israel (Luke 13:6). This then was the asked for sign. Israel, He said, would soon be destroyed (Matt. 24:1-2), and when she began to bloom again the Second Coming would then be very near! He furthermore added that the generation of Israelites born during that blossom-time period would still be alive to see the Second Advent!

Some forty years after this sermon was given, Jerusalem was completely destroyed by the Roman general Titus in 70 A.D. Since that time, the fig tree of Israel has stood alone, without fruit and almost without hope.

There have been many important dates in history since Jesus ascended into heaven. In 324 Constantine came into full power and made Christianity the state religion. In 476 the Roman Empire fell. In 1054 the Eastern and Western Christian Church split. On August 3, 1492, Columbus set sail. On July 4, 1776 the American Declaration of Independence was signed. On August 6, 1945, the first atomic bomb was dropped on Japan. Finally, on July 20, 1969, man first walked on the moon! But in my opinion the most important date during the past twenty centuries occurred on May 14, 1948. It was on that day at 4:30 P.M. that Israel officially became a nation again! In his book, *Abraham to the Middle East Crisis,* Dr. G. Frederick Owen writes of this:

> Early that morning Great Britain's flag, the Union Jack was hauled down. During that sunny day a multitude gathered at a roped-off, guarded section of Rothchild Boulevard in Tel Aviv (the new Capital). The chief Rabbi leaders along with

many representatives of the world press awaited. At exactly 4 P.M., David BenGurion called the meeting to order. The Assembly rose and sang the Jewish National Anthem, "Hatikvah,' while in an adjoining room the Palestinian Symphony Orchestra played. The music had hardly ceased when Ben-Gurion rose and read in a firm voice in Hebrew, the Declaration of Independence of the new nation Israel. The entire assemblage rose and applauded, and many of them wept.[33]

On February 1, 1949, the United States recognized Israel, and in May of that same year Israel became the fifty-ninth member of the United Nations!

11. The absence of charismatic leadership

Some eleven centuries B.C., Israel's elders approached their old judge, Samuel, and demanded, "Give us a king to judge us" (1 Sam. 8:6)! This has always been and continues to be the cry of mankind. Give us a leader to guide us and a cause to challenge us!

In the fullness of time therefore (Gal. 4:4), God sent this perfect leader. But the world rejected Him (John 1:10-11). As a result, Jesus Christ predicted that someday sinful mankind would receive a false king (John 5:43). In Revelation 13, the apostle John predicted also that this wicked and depraved dictator (often called the Antichrist) would demand and receive the obedience and worship of this earth!

The point of all the above is simply this: If the end is really close, then the stage should be set for such a king. Is there among the nations today a vacuum of charismatic leadership?

By definition, a charismatic person is a gifted leader. But he is far more than that. He possesses some strange and invisible (but very real) "personality perfume" which can immediately excite and inspire followers. Some leaders have this; some do not. The Kennedys possessed it. It was referred to by the news media as "that Kennedy magic." We note, however, the demise or death of many such charismatic leaders in recent years.

G. Prophecies fulfilled by our Lord during His earthly ministry

In the Old Testament there are some thirty-seven basic prophecies concerning the earthly ministry of the anticipated Saviour. While upon this earth, Jesus Christ fulfilled every single prediction! Consider the following texts:

1. He would be born of a virgin—compare Isa. 7:14 with Matt. 1:22, 23.
2. He would be given the throne of David—compare 2 Sam. 7:12, 13 with Luke 1:31.
3. He would be called Emmanuel—compare Isa. 7:14 with Matt. 1:23.
4. He would be rejected by His own—Compare Isa. 53: 3 with John 1:11; 7:5.
5. He would have a forerunner—Compare Isa. 40:3-5; Mal. 3:1, with Luke 1:76-78; 3:3-6; Matt. 3:1-3.
6. He would be born in Bethlehem—compare Micah 5:2-3 with Matt. 2:5-6.
7. He would be visited by the magi and presented with gifts—Compare Isa. 60:3, 6, 9, with Matt. 2:11.
8. He would be in Egypt for a season—compare Hos. 11:1 with Matt. 2:15.
9. His birthplace would suffer a massacre of infants—compare Jer. 31:5 with Matt. 2:17-18.
10. He would be called a Nazarene—compare Isa. 11:1 with Matt. 2:23.
11. He would be zealous for His Father—compare Ps. 69:9 with John 2:13-17.
12. He would be filled with God's Spirit—compare Isa. 61: 1-3; 11:2 with Luke 4:18-19.
13. He would be a light to the Gentiles—compare Isa. 42: 1-3, 6-7 with Matt. 4:13-16; 12:18-21.
14. He would heal many—compare Isa. 53:4 with Matt. 8: 16-17.
15. He would deal gently with the Gentiles—compare Isa. 9:1-2; 42:1-3 with Matt. 12:17-21.
16. He would speak in parables—compare Isa. 6:9, 10 with Matt. 13:10-15.
17. He would make a triumphal entry into Jerusalem—Compare Zech. 9:9 with Matt. 21:4-5.
18. He would be praised by little children—compare Ps. 8:2 with Matt. 21:16.
19. He would be the rejected cornerstone—compare Ps. 118: 22, 23 with Matt. 21:42.
20. His miracles would not be believed—compare Isa. 53:1 with John 12:37-38.

21. His friend would betray Him for thirty pieces of silver—Compare Ps. 41:9; 55:12-14; Zech. 11:12, 13 with Matt. 26:14-16, 21-25.
22. He would be a man of sorrows—compare Isa. 53:3 with Matt. 26:37-38.
23. He would be forsaken by His disciples—compare Zech. 13:7 with Matt. 26:31, 56.
24. He would be scourged and spat upon—compare Isa. 50:6 with Matt. 26:67; 27:26.
25. His price-money would be used to buy a potter's field—compare Zech. 11:12, 13; Jer. 18:1-4; 19:1-3 with Matt. 27:9-10.
26. He would be crucified between two thieves—compare Isa. 53:12 with Matt. 27:38; Mark 15:27-28; Luke 22:37.
27. He would be given vinegar to drink—compare Ps. 69:21 with Matt. 27:34, 48.
28. He would suffer the piercing of His hands and feet—compare Ps. 22:16; Zech. 12:10 with Mark 15:25; John 19:34, 37; 20:25-27.
29. His garments would be parted and gambled for—compare Ps. 22:18 with Luke 23:34; John 19:23, 24.
30. He would be surrounded and ridiculed by His enemies—compare Ps. 22:7-8 with Matt. 27:39-44; Mark 15:29-32.
31. He would thirst—compare Ps. 22:15 with John 19:28.
32. He would commend His spirit to the Father—compare Ps. 31:5 with Luke 23:46.
33. His bones would not be broken—compare Ps. 34:20; Exod. 12:46; Num. 9:12 with John 19:33-36.
34. He would be stared at in death—compare Zech. 12:10 with John 19:37; Matt. 27:36.
35. He would be buried with the rich—compare Isa. 59:9 with Matt. 27:57-60.
36. He would be raised from the dead—compare Ps. 16:10 with Matt. 28:2-7.
37. He would ascend—compare Ps. 24:7-10 with Mark 16:19; Luke 24:50.

VI. Sixth Supernatural Element—Its Universal Influence!

A. Upon civilization

1. Western civilization is founded directly upon the Bible and its teachings. Its very manner of life had its origin in Acts 16:9, when Paul, obedient to his heavenly vision, directed his second missionary journey towards Europe instead of Asia and the East!
2. The world's calendar and most of its holidays stem from the Bible.
3. It was the Bible which elevated the blood-drinking savages of the British Isles to decency.
4. The Bible has influenced, if not directed, the advancement of all fine arts.
   a. Literature
   Ruskin quotes over 5,000 scriptural references in his writings. Milton's greatest works are rooted in the Word of God, as are Shakespeare's and others such as Coleridge, Scott, Pope, Bryant, Longfellow, Kipling, Caryle, MaCaulay, Hawthorne, Irving, Thoreau, and others.
   b. Art
   Over fifty-two world-famous paintings depicting well-known scenes in the Old Testament, along with over sixty-five in the New Testament are preserved today. These paintings can be found in every important museum on earth. They have been done by the greatest and most talented artists of all time. These would include Leonardo da Vinci, Rembrandt, Raphael, Michelangelo, and others.
   c. Music
   The Bible has produced more inspiring music than all other combined books in the world.
   Bach—History has concluded that Johann Sebastian Bach "anticipated every important (musical) idea that has been born since his day. He is the inspiration of the pianist, the organist, and the composer." Bach was a zealous Lutheran who devoted most of his genius to Bible church-centered music.
   Mendelssohn—Author of "St. Paul, Elijah"
   Brahms—Requiem
   Beethoven—Mt. of Olives, Samson and Delilah
   Handel—The Messiah (he quotes from fifteen books of the Bible)
   Haydn—The Creation
5. The Bible has produced the law of the Western world.

Early attempts of governing forms such as the English common law, the Bill of Rights, the Magna Carta, and our own Constitution are all rooted in God's gift to Moses on Mt. Sinai, the Ten Commandments.

B. Upon America

1. The Bible led to the discovery of our country. According to a written statement from his own pen, Columbus testified it was certain texts in Isaiah that prompted his fateful trip in 1492. He later wrote, "In the Name of the most Holy Trinity who inspired me with the idea and afterwards made it perfectly clear to me that I could go to the Indies from Spain by traversing the ocean westwardly."

2. It was Bible lovers desiring to read this blessed Book in personal freedom who populated our shores. There were the Puritans in England, the Huguenots in France, the Dunkers in Germany, and the Anabaptists from all over Europe who came here. The Pilgrims came to Plymouth Rock in 1620 because of the Bible.

3. The charter of every colony includes Bible language—

a. *Salem*—"We covenant with the Lord . . . to walk together in all His ways . . . as He has revealed . . . in His blessed word of truth."

b. *Rhode Island*—"We submit . . . to the Lord Jesus Christ, the King of Kings and the Lord of Lords."

c. *Delaware*—"For the further propagation of the Holy Gospel."

d. *Maryland*—"A pious zeal for extending the Christian religion."

e. *Massachusetts*—"To the knowledge and obedience of the only true God and the Saviour of mankind."

f. *Connecticut*—"To preserve the liberty and purity of the Gospel of our Lord Jesus Christ."

As one considers the almost desperate (and often vicious) attempts on the part of God from all American educational and political systems, he is forced to this painful conclusion: The actual establishment of the original thirteen colonies would have been strictly prohibited under existing laws today! Thus one atheist owes the very rights she enjoys today in the state of Maryland to those "narrow-minded Puritan bigots," whose love for God and freedom she so passionately hates! It is indeed a strange world!

4. Less than 1 percent of the total adult population in 1776 were not members of a Protestant church.

5. The American Revolution was produced by the Bible—The Liberty Bell itself bears a scriptural injunction—"proclaim liberty throughout all the land unto the inhabitants thereof" (Lev. 25:10). Even today our most important capitol buildings and monuments display scriptural truths. These include: the Capitol building, the Supreme Court building, the White House, the Library of Congress, The Washington Monument, The Thomas Jefferson Memorial, The Lincoln Memorial, The Tomb of the Unknown Soldier, The Union Station and others. Every single charter of the fifty United States includes the word God, and other biblical phrases.

6. Our presidents are still sworn into their high office by placing their right hand on an ancient book, THE BIBLE.

7. American education has its roots in the Bible. The New England Primer was a Bible primer. In 1642 Massachusetts law required schools to operate. The stated reason was: "It being one chief project of that old deluder Satan to keep men from the knowledge of the Scriptures." Of the ten first colleges in America, nine were founded by churches, and the tenth by evangelist George Whitfield. Ninety-five percent of the colleges and universities in America today were founded by Christian bodies. In 1780 Robert Raikes in England initiated the Sunday school movement, which led to the establishment of the American public school system.

8. Abraham Lincoln's Gettysburg Address was inspired by John Wycliffe's introduction to the New Testament when he wrote: "The Bible is for the government of the people, by the people, and for the people."

9. Julia Ward Howe's great Civil War song, *Mine Eyes Have Seen the Glory,* was taken from the pages of the Bible. Other patriotic songs are likewise grounded in biblical terms, such as *The Star-Spangled Banner,* by Frances Scott Key; *America the Beautiful,* by Katherine Lee Bates, and others.

10. American altruism (humanitarianism) has been originated by those people who have loved the message of the Bible. This would include:

a. reforms in penal systems.
b. reforms in child labor injustices.
c. reforms in mental institutions.
d. creation of mercy organizations such as the Salvation Army, YMCA, YWCA, crippled children's associations, homes for the aged, orphanages, rescue missions, etc. Since our beginning as a nation, we have donated over 50 billion dollars to practically every nation in the world for the purposes of good will, and in many cases, to stave off mass starvation.
e. The modern nursing system is taken from Luke 10:30-37, the parable of the Good Samaritan.
f. The symbol of the medical profession is a coiling serpent, taken from Num. 21:8, 9.

VII. Seventh Supernatural Element—Its Care and Copy!

A. No book in history has been copied as many times with as much care as has been the Word of God. The Talmud lists the following rules for copying the Old Testament:

1. The parchment had to be made from the skin of a clean animal, prepared by a Jew only, and must be fastened by strings from clean animals.

2. Each column must have no less than forty-eight or more than sixty lines.

3. The ink must be of no other color than black, and had to be prepared according to a special recipe.

4. No word nor letter could be written from memory; the scribe must have an authentic copy before him, and he had to read and pronounce aloud each word before writing it.

5. He had to reverently wipe his pen each time before writing the Word of God, and had to wash his whole body before writing the sacred name Jehovah!

6. One mistake on a sheet condemned the sheet; if three mistakes were found on any page, the entire manuscript was condemned.

7. Every word and every letter was counted, and if a letter were omitted, an extra letter inserted, or if one letter touched another, the manuscript was condemned and destroyed at once.

The old rabbi gave the solemn warning to each young scribe: "Take heed how thou dost do thy work, for thy work is the work of heaven; lest thou drop or add a letter of a manuscript and so become a destroyer of the world!"

The scribe was also told that while he was writing if even a king would enter the room and speak with him, the scribe was to ignore him until he finished the page he were working on,lest he make a mistake! In fact, some texts were actually annotated—that is, each letter was individually counted! Thus in copying the Old Testament they would note the letter aleph (first letter in the Hebrew alphabet) occured 42,377 times, and so on.

According to Westcott and Hort, the points in which we cannot be sure of the original words are microscopic in proportion to the bulk of the whole, some 1/1000. Thus only one letter out of 1,580 in the Old Testament is open to question, and none of these uncertainties would change in the slightest any doctrinal teaching!

B. Today there are almost 5,000 ancient Greek manuscripts of the New Testament. This perhaps does not seem like many, until one considers that—

1. Fifteen hundred years after Herodotus wrote his history there was only one copy in the entire world.

2. Twelve hundred years after Plato wrote his classic, there was only one manuscript.

3. Today there exist but a few manuscripts of Sophocles, Euripedes, Virgil, and Cicero.

VIII. Eighth Supernatural Element—Its Amazing Circulation!

When David Hume said, "I see the twilight of Christianity and the Bible," he was much confused, for he could not tell the sunrise from the sunset! Consider the following facts about this amazing Book:

A. The American Bible Society has distributed 850 million Bibles since 1816.

B. At least one book of the Bible is now in 1,250 languages.

C. The Bible in its completeness is now in 237 languages.

D. At present there are more than 3,000 translators working in 150 countries translating the Word of God!

E. Only one-half of one percent of all books published survive seven years. Eighty percent of all books are forgotten in one year. For example, let us imagine that during this year, 200 new books are published in America. Statistics show that by next year only 40 of these 200 will remain. At the end of the seventh year, of the original 200, only one lonely book will survive!

F. Scripture distribution has increased 200 percent over 1960, according to the ABS.

G. A new $5.5 million twelve-story building has recently been completed which will function as the new headquarters for the ABS!

H. During the Civil War, the ABS produced 7,000 Bibles a day for both sides! When Grant's armies marched through Tennessee, horse-drawn Bible vans followed. In 1864, the Memphis Bible Society sent a shipment of cotton to New York in return for 50,000 Scripture portions.

What other ancient religious book can even remotely be compared to all this? Where could one go today to purchase a copy of Zen Vedas, or the Egyptian Book of the Dead? In fact, dozens of religions which once flourished have simply disappeared from the face of the earth without leaving the slightest trace. Other ancient religions may be viewed behind glass cases in the rare book section of dusty museums. But the smallest child can walk into almost any dime store in America and pick up a copy of the Word of God!

IX. Ninth Supernatural Element—Its Absolute Honesty!

Perhaps no other single statement so completely summarizes the Bible as does the following: "The Bible is not a Book that man *could* write if he would, or *would* write if he could!" Let us analyze this one section at a time.

Man could not write the Bible if he would—Even if a man had all the necessary spirituality he could not know the facts involved in the historical, scientific, and prophetical statements we have previously already seen in the Bible. Thus, without God's direction the Bible is not a Book that man could write if he would!

Man would not write the Bible if he could—Suppose God would give sinful man all the necessary facts and abilities to write the Bible. What then? Man still *would* not write it correctly if he *could!* Note the following reasons:

A. Because of the bad things God writes about some of His friends. Here five men immediately come to mind. Most of these individuals are mentioned in the Faith Hall of Fame (Hebrews 11).

1. Noah—indeed a man of God! He walketh with God; he was a just man (Gen. 6:9), and he obeyed God (Heb. 11:7)! Yet after the Flood this great hero of the faith gets dead drunk and exposes his nakedness and shame to his entire family (Gen. 9:20-24). Surely a mere human author would not have written all this!

2. Moses—the meekest man in all the earth during his time (Num. 12:3), and a leader who single-handedly led an entire nation of enslaved Hebrews out of captivity in Egypt. But en route to Palestine we read of his anger and direct disobedience to the clearly revealed Word of God! (See Num. 20:7-12). Surely man would have eliminated this part of Moses' record.

3. David—without exception the grandest human king whoever sat upon a throne! God Himself would testify that here was a man after His own heart (see 1 Sam. 13:14; 16:7, 12, 13). David's fearlessness (1 Sam. 17:34-36, 49), love for God (Ps. 18, 103, etc.), and kindness (1 Sam. 24:6-7) was universally known. But in 2 Samuel 11 this same king is accurately accused of lust, adultery, lying, and cold-blooded murder! Who but God would write in such a manner?

4. Elijah—few other Old Testament prophets are as colorful and exciting as Elijah the Tishbite. In 1 Kings 18, he champions the cause of Christ against 450 priests of Satan, but in the very next chapter he is pictured as running for his very life from a mere woman!

5. Peter—self-appointed spokesman for Christ who so confidently assured the Savior that, "Though all men shall be offended because of Thee, yet will I never be offended" (Matt. 26:33). But in the hour of Jesus' great need we read of Peter: "Then began he to curse and to swear, saying, I know not the man" (Matt. 26:74).

B. Because of the good things God writes about some of His enemies.

In the TV series, the bad guys wear black hats and never do anything good, while the good guys wear white hats and rarely do anything wrong! But not in the Bible! As we have already seen, on many occasions God records bad things about the white hats, and He often mentions good things about the black hats. This can be seen in the account of *Esau* (Genesis 33); *Artaxerxes* (Nehemiah 2); *Darius* (Daniel 6); *Gamaliel* (Acts 5:34-39); *Julius* (Acts 27:1-3); etc.

The point of all the above is simply this—the Bible is *not* an edited Book! God literally "tells it like it is." Human authors, however sincere, simply do not consistently write this way!

C. Because of certain doctrines repugnant to the natural mind. Many examples could be listed here, but the following three will demonstrate this:

1. The doctrine of eternal hell! (See Rev. 14:10-11.)
2. The doctrine of man's total helplessness! (See Eph. 2:8-9; Rom. 7:18.)
3. The doctrine of final judgment upon saved and unsaved! (See 1 Cor. 3:9-15; Rev. 20:11-15.)

X. Tenth Supernatural Element—Its Life-Transforming Power!

According to an ancient proverb—"The proof of the pudding is in the eating." So it is. Undoubtedly the greatest proof of all that the Bible is indeed God's Word is its amazing ability to change corrupt humanity!

It is said that a socialist once stood on a soap box in New York and, pointing to an old ragged bum, proudly announced, "Socialism will put a new suit of clothes on that old man there."

As he stepped down, a Christian mounted the box and proclaimed, "The Bible will put a new man in that old suit of clothes there."

An atheist once sneeringly asked a new convert the question, "Do you believe Jesus actually turned water into wine?" The convert answered: "Yes, I believe He did! But let me tell you something. For years I was a hopeless drunkard. All my money went for booze. But then God's Word gripped my soul and I'm here to say that Jesus performed an even greater miracle, for He turned wine into milk for my children!"

The following are but a few examples among the multiplied millions which could be offered to demonstrate the power of this Book of God.

A. As illustrated by author H. L. Hastings:

> Years ago a young infidel and his uncle, a banker, were traveling in the West. They were a little anxious for their safety when they were forced to stop for the night in a rough wayside cabin. There were two rooms in the house, and when they retired for the night, they agreed that the young man should sit with his pistol, and watch until midnight and then awaken his uncle who would watch until morning. Presently, he peeped through the crack of the partition and saw his host, a rough-looking old man in his bear-skin suit, reach up and take down a book, the Bible, and after reading awhile, he knelt and began to pray. Then the young infidel began to pull off his coat and get ready for bed. The uncle said, "I thought you were going to sit up and watch," but the young man knew there was no need of sitting up, pistol in hand, to watch all night long in a cabin that was hallowed by the Word of God, and consecrated by the voice of prayer. Would a pack of cards, a rum bottle, or a copy of Age of Reason have thus quieted this young infidel's fears? [34]

B. As illustrated by Henry Stanley:

> Why is it that, when Henry Stanley journeyed into the tangled forest of Africa to find David Livingstone, he started out with one hundred-eighty pounds of books, but as hunger and illness forced the sacrifice of unessentials, he discarded volume after volume until all he had was an edition of Shakespeare,

a copy of Carlyle, two treatises on navigation, and the Bible; and concerning these five books he said on his return to the United States, 'Poor Shakespeare was afterwards burned up; Carlyle and the navigation books were abandoned by the way, and I had only the Bible left!" During this time, Stanley read his Bible through three times. He is quoted as follows: "During my first attack of African fever, I took up the Bible to while away the tedious hours. I read Job, and then the Psalms. Its powerful verses had a different meaning in the silence of the wilds. I came to feel a strange glow . . . Alone in my tent I flung myself on my knees and poured out my soul utterly in secret prayer to Him. . . .[35]

C. As illustrated by Captain Bligh:

Probably there is no more sensational example of the life-transforming power of the Bible than the unbelievable story of Mutiny on the Bounty. In 1887 the Bounty, under Captain Bligh, set sail for the island of Tahiti in the South Seas. After a voyage of ten months, the ship arrived at her destination, and further six months were spent collecting palm saplings. The sailors meanwhile had become so attached to the native girls, that upon receiving the order to embark, mutinied, set the Captain and a few men adrift in an open boat, and returned to the island. Captain Bligh, however, survived his ordeal and eventually arrived home in England. A punitive expedition was sent out, which captured 14 of the mutineers. But nine of them had transferred to another island, where they formed a new colony. Here, in the language of the Encyclopedia Britannica, they degenerated so fast and became so fierce as to make the life of the colony a hell on earth. The chief reason for this was the distillation of whiskey from a native plant. Quarrels, orgies, and murders were a common feature of their life. Finally all the men except one were killed or had died off. Alexander Smith was left alone with a crowd of native women and half-breed children. Then a strange thing happened. In a battered chest, he found a Bible. He read it, believed it, and began to live it. Determining to make amends for his past evil life, he gathered the women and children around him and taught them too. Time rolled on. The children grew up and became Christians. The community prospered exceedingly. Nearly 20 years later an American ship visited the island and brought back to Europe and England word of its peaceful state. The British government took no further action. There was no need. The island was a Christian community. There was no disease, no insanity, no crime, and no illiteracy, and no strong drink. Life and property were safe, and the moral standards of the people were as high as anywhere in the world. It was a veritable Utopia on a small scale. What had brought about this astounding transformation? Just the reading of a book, and that book was the Bible. [36]

D. As illustrated by Billy Graham:

Among the many thousands of conversions in the London Crusade were those of a medical doctor and the man who sat next to him in the arena. Before the service began, the two strangers engaged in conversation, criticizing the campaign and expressing the utmost skepticism. As Graham preached, throwing out one truth of Scripture after another, the doctor was gripped by an unseen power. When the invitation was given, he said to the man next to him. "I don't know about you, but I'm going forward to receive Christ." The other hesitated a moment, then reached into his pocket and replied, "I'm going too, and here's your wallet. I'm a pickpocket." [37]

E. As illustrated by Captain Mitsuo Fuchida:

When Captain Mitsuo Fuchida, the Japanese squadron commander who led the air raid on Pearl Harbor in 1941, and Jacob DeShazer, one of the famed Doolittle flyers who participated in the bombing of Tokyo in 1942, sat on a platform together in Christian evangelistic meetings in Japan they created a great sensation. And so they should! Bitter national enemies who had delighted in sending fiery death and destruction to each other, were united in a tremendous cooperative effort for Christian evangelism.[38]

F. As illustrated by Gypsy Smith:

When the famous evangelist, Gypsy Smith, was holding a series of meetings in Chicago in 1923, a young man who had been born and reared in the most profane and evil kind of environment carried a brick to one of the services for the purpose of winning a bet. He intended to throw the brick at the evangelist, start a riot, and break up the meeting. When Gypsy Smith walked on the platform, his attention was immediately drawn to the depraved man sitting near the front of the theater. Looking him straight in the face, he said with conviction, 'Young man, Jesus loves you!' and began to preach the Word of God. The brick was never thrown. The next morning the ruffian visited the evangelist's hotel room, still carrying the brick. With great emotion he told of his purpose the night before, and of the experience that had prevented his fulfilling it. The Word of God, like a knife, had gone straight to his wicked heart and left him shaken, miserable, and helpless. After telling his story, he dropped to his knees beside the evangelist and prayed with a strange mingling of profanity and obscenity, the only language he knew. Three years later, in his home in England, Gypsy Smith received a Christmas Card greeting signed by sixteen students who had just graduated from the Moody Bible Institute. The first name on the list was that of the young man who had carried the brick.[39]

G. As illustrated by Augustine:

Shortly after his new birth experience, Augustine met a prostitute on the street. Pretending not to see her, he attempted to pass by without recognition, but she called, "Augustine, it is I." He turned to her then and answered, "Yes, but it is not I!" [40]

H. As illustrated by Sir Walter Scott:

There is not a more familiar story in the annals of literature than the story that describes the death of the immortal Scot poet and novelist, Sir Walter Scott. As he lay dying he turned to his son-in-law, Lockhart, and said to him, "Son, bring me the Book." There was a vast library in Walter Scott's home and bewildered, the son-in-law said, "Sir, what book?" "Which book?" The dying bard replied, "My son, there is just one Book. Bring me the Book." It is then that Lockhart went to the library and brought to Sir Walter Scott the Bible!

"There's just one book," cried the dying sage,
"Read me the old, old story."
And the winged words that can never age
Wafted him home to glory.
There's just one Book.

There's just one book for the tender years,
One book alone for guiding,
—The little feet through the joys and fears,
The unknown days are hiding
There's just one Book!

There's just one book for the bridal hour,
One book of love's own coining,
Its truths alone lend beauty and power,

To vows that lives are joining.
There's just one book!

—There's just one book for life's gladness,
One book for the toilsome days.
One book that can cure life's madness,
One book that can voice life's praise.
There's just one Book!

There's just one book for the dying,
One book for the starting tears,
And one for the soul that is going home,
For the measureless years.
There's just one Book! [41]

There is indeed but one Book!

I. As illustrated by the apostle Paul

According to his own testimony, Paul was the "chief of sinners" (1 Tim. 1:13). To show this was no empty claim, Paul sadly relates his pre-Christian sinful activities:

1. He took care of the coats of Stephen's murderers as they stoned him (Acts 8:3).
2. He arrested Christians and threw them into prison (Acts 8:3; 22:4).
3. He beat Christians (Acts 22:19).
4. He compelled them to use abusive language (Acts 26:11).
5. He persecuted them unto death (Acts 22:4).
6. He attempted to destroy the Christian faith (Gal. 1:23).
7. He wasted the church of God and made havoc of it (Gal. 1:13; Acts 8:3). This word "havoc" occurs but once here in the Greek New Testament and refers to a wild boar which charges into a vineyard and viciously uproots it!

But then this ravaging wolf heard the voice of the Shepherd and became one of God's best sheepdogs!

Most Americans are aware of the perverted poison of the notorious atheist Madalyn Murray O'Hare, well-known atheist. This person, like most atheists, finds a fiendish glee in ridiculing Christians and the Christian faith. "That pie-in-the-sky is a great big lie!" they sneer. But what do they offer in place of Christ and the Bible? The following statements come from the mouths of various atheists:

Byron—"Count o'er the joys thine hours have seen, Count o'er thy days from anguish free, And know, whatever thou hast been, Tis something better not to be." [42]

Ingersoll—"For, whether in mid-sea or among the breakers of the farther shore, a wreck must mark at last the end of each and all. And every life, no matter if its every hour is rich with love and every moment jeweled with a joy, will, at its close, become a tragedy, as sad, and deep, and dark as can be woven of the warp and woof of mystery and death. Life is a narrow vale between the cold and barren peaks of two eternities. We strive in vain to look beyond the heights. We cry aloud, and the only answer is the echo of our wailing cry. From the voiceless lips of the unreplying dead there comes no word." [43]

Strauss—"In the enormous machine of the universe, amid wheel and hiss of its jagged iron wheels, amid the deafening clash of its stamps and hammers, in the midst of this whole terrific commotion, man finds himself placed with no security for a moment, that a wheel might not seize and render him, or a hammer crash him to pieces." [44]

Anatole France—" 'In all the world the unhappiest creature is man.' He takes my hands in his and his are trembling and feverish. He looks me in the eyes. His are full of tears. His face is haggard. He sighs: 'There is not in all the universe a creature more unhappy than I. People think me happy. I have never been happy for one day, not for a single hour.' " [45]

Bertrand Russell—"The life of Man is a long march through the night, surrounded by invisible foes, tortured by weariness and pain, towards a goal that few can hope to reach, and where none may tarry long." [46]

Mark Twain—"A myriad of men are born; they scramble for little mean advantages over each other; age creeps upon them and infirmities follow; shame and humiliations bring down their prides and vanities. Those they love are taken from them and the joy of life is turned into aching grief. The burden of pain, care, misery, grows heavier year by year. At length ambition is dead, pride is dead, vanity is dead; longing for release is in their place. It comes at last—the only unpoisoned gift earth ever had for them—and they vanish from a world where they were of no consequence, where they left no sign that they have existed—a world that will lament them for a day and forget them forever." [47]

Schopenhauer—"Life is necessarily and hopelessly wretched. To live is to desire, to desire is to want, to want is to suffer, and hence to live is to suffer. No man is happy except when drunk or deluded; his happiness is only like that of a beggar who dreams that he is a king. Nothing is worth the trouble which it costs us. Wretchedness always outweighs felicity. The history of man is a long, confused, and painful dream." [48]

Charles Darwin—"I have everything to make me happy and contented, but life has become very wearisome to me." [49]

Teller—"As the sun loses weight at the rate of more than four million tons a second, its gravitational hold is rapidly decreasing, and we are each year headed, in an ever-increasing spiral course, toward the great, yawning abyss beyond. While there is no immediate danger of our being swept into oblivion, the time will arrive when all earthly things will be doomed to perish, when the earth will be too cold to sustain life, and the finest of human thoughts will have been lost forever. Then our earth, like all things else, will have joined the billions of lifeless globes." [50]

Thus is life without the God of the Bible! As we conclude this section and the book itself, the words of the familiar song come to mind:

THE B-I-B-L-E! YES, THAT'S THE BOOK FOR ME!
I STAND ALONE ON THE WORD OF GOD—
THE B-I-B-L-E!

THE BIBLE is a beautiful palace built of sixty-six blocks of solid marble—the sixty-six books. In the first chapter of *Genesis* we enter the vestibule, filled with the mighty acts of creation.

The vestibule gives access to the law courts—the *five books of Moses*—passing through which we come to the picture gallery of the *historical* books. Here we find hung upon the walls scenes of battlefields, representations of heroic deeds, and portraits of eminent men belonging to the early days of the world's history.

Beyond the picture gallery we find the philosopher's chamber —the book of *Job*—passing through which we enter the music room—the book of *Psalms*—where we listen to the grandest strains that ever fell on human ears.

Then we come to the business office—the book of *Proverbs*— where right in the center of the room, stands facing us the motto, "Righteousness exalteth a nation, but sin is a reproach to any people."

From the business office we pass into the chapel—*Ecclesiastes,* or the *Song of Solomon* with the rose of sharon and the lily of the valley, and all manner of fine perfume and fruit and flowers and singing birds.

Finally we reach the observatory—the *Prophets,* with their telescopes fixed on near and distant stars, and all directed toward "the Bright and Morning Star," that was soon to arise.

Crossing the court we come to the audience chamber of the King—the *Gospels*—where we find four vivid life-like portraits of the King Himself. Next we enter the work-room of the Holy Spirit—the *Acts of the Apostles*—and beyond that the correspondence room—the *Epistles*—where we see Paul and Peter and James and John and Jude busy at their desks.

Before leaving we stand a moment in the outside gallery— the *Revelation*—where we look upon some striking pictures of the judgments to come, and the glories to be revealed, concluding with an awe-inspiring picture of the throne room of the King.

THE FORTY-EIGHT MOST IMPORTANT CHAPTERS IN THE OLD TESTAMENT

Compiled by H. L. Willmington

The Old Testament has 929 chapters. The following forty-eight chapters have been selected because of their historical, prophetical, theological, or practical significance.

GENESIS
- 1—Creation of all things
- 3—Fall of man
- 6—The Universal Flood
- 11—The Tower of Babel
- 12—The Call of Abraham
- 15—The Confirmation of the Abrahamic Covenant

EXODUS
- 3—The Call of Moses
- 12—The Passover
- 14—The Red Sea Crossing
- 16—The Giving of the Sabbath
- 20—The Giving of the Law
- 40—The Completion of the Tabernacle

LEVITICUS
- 8—The Anointing of Aaron as Israel's First High Priest
- 23—The Feasts of Israel

NUMBERS
- 14—The Rebellion at Kadesh-barnea
- 21—The Serpent of Brass

DEUTERONOMY
- 28—Israel's Future Predicted by Moses

JOSHUA
- 4—Israel Enters the Promised Land

RUTH
- 4—The Marriage of Boaz and Ruth

I SAMUEL
- 9—The Anointing of Saul as Israel's First King
- 16—The Anointing of David

II SAMUEL
- 6—Jerusalem becomes the Capital of Israel
- 7—The Giving of the Davidic Covenant

I KINGS

8—The Dedication of the Temple by Solomon
12—The Divided Kingdom of Israel

II KINGS

17—The Capture of the Northern Kingdom by Assyria
19—The Saving of Jerusalem by the Death Angel
24—The Capture of the Southern Kingdom by Babylon

EZRA

1—The Decree of Cyrus and the Return to Jerusalem

JOB

1—The Confrontations between God and Satan (see also Job 2)

PSALMS

22—The Psalm of Calvary
23—The Psalm of the Good Shepherd
51—The Great Confession of Sin Chapter
119—The Psalm of the Word of God

ISAIAH

7—The Prophecy of the Virgin Birth
14—The Fall of Satan
35—The Millennium
53—The Sufferings of Christ

JEREMIAH

31—The Promise of the New Covenant to Israel

EZEKIEL

10—The Departure of the Glory Cloud from Israel
28—The Pre-historical life of Satan
37—The Dry Bone Vision of Israel's Restoration
38—The Future Russian Invasion into Palestine (see also Ezekiel 39)
40—The Future Millennial Temple

DANIEL

2—The Dream of the Future Gentile World Powers (see also Daniel 7)
9—The Vision of the Seventy Weeks

JONAH

2—The Great Fish and Jonah

ZECHARIAH

14—The Second Coming of Christ

THE FIFTY-THREE MOST IMPORTANT CHAPTERS IN THE NEW TESTAMENT

Compiled by H. L. Willmington

The New Testament has 260 chapters. The following fifty-three chapters have been selected because of their historical, prophetical, theological, or practical significance.

MATTHEW

3—The Baptism of Jesus
4—The Temptation of Jesus
5—The Sermon on the Mount
6—The Lord's Prayer
13—The Parable of the Sower
16—The Promise of the Church
17—The Transfiguration of Jesus
21—The Rejection of Israel by Jesus
27—The Crucifixion of Jesus
28—The Resurrection of Jesus

LUKE

1—The Birth of John the Baptist
2—The Birth of Jesus

JOHN

2—The First Miracle of Jesus
3—Jesus and Nicodemus
11—The Resurrection of Lazarus
13—The Lord's Supper
14—The Father's House Sermon
15—The Abiding Chapter
17—The Prayer of Jesus

ACTS

1—The Ascension of Jesus
2—Pentecost
9—The Conversion of Saul
13—The Call of Saul and Barnabas
15—The Jerusalem Council
16—The Macedonial Vision

ROMANS

5—The Justification Chapter
6—The Sanctification Chapter
8—The Glorification Chapter

11—The Dispensation Chapter
12—The Consecration Chapter

I CORINTHIANS

3—The Judgment Seat of Christ
7—The Marriage Chapter
11—Teachings on the Lord's Supper
12—The Gifts of the Spirit
13—The Love Chapter
14—The Tongue Chapter
15—The Resurrection Chapter

GALATIANS

5—The Fruit of the Spirit

EPHESIANS

5—The Love of Christ for His Church
6—The Protection of the Believer

PHILIPPIANS

2—The Kenosis (Emptying) of Christ

I THESSALONIANS

4—The Rapture

II TIMOTHY

3—Duties of Pastors and Deacons

HEBREWS

11—Faith Chapter
12—Chastisement Chapter

JAMES

3—Gossip Chapter

I JOHN

1—Fellowship Chapter

JUDE

1—Apostasy Chapter

REVELATION

6—Beginning of Tribulation
13—The Ministry of the Antichrist
19—Second Coming of Christ
20—Great White Throne Judgment
21—New Heaven and New Earth

Footnotes

[1] Charles Hodge, *Systematic Theology* (Grand Rapids: Eerdmans Publishing Co., 1940), Vol. I, p. 157.
[2] Charles F. Baker, *A Dispensational Theology* (Grand Rapids: Grace Bible College Publications, 1971), p. 38.
[3] From a news release of Dr. Harold J. Ockenga, December 8, 1957.
[4] Leo Rosten, *A Guide to the Religions of America* (New York: Simon and Schuster, Inc., 1955), p. 152.
[5] Vernon C. Grounds, *The Reason for Our Hope* (Chicago: Moody Press, 1945), p. 67.
[6] Rosten, *Guide to Religions*, p. 23.
[7] John B. Wilder, *The Other Side of Rome* (Grand Rapids: Zondervan Publishing House, 1959), pp. 112-113.
[8] Norman Geisler and William Nix, *A General Introduction to the Bible* (Chicago: Moody Press, 1968), pp. 219-220.
[9] *Ibid.*, p. 221.
[10] Merrill F. Unger, *Unger's Bible Handbook* (Chicago: Moody Press, 1966), p. 459.
[11] H. S. Miller, *General Biblical Introduction* (Houghton, N.Y.: The Word-Bearer Press, 1952), p. 320.
[12] *Ibid.*, p. 321.
[13] *Ibid.*, p. 363-364.
[14] Unger, *Handbook*, p. 893.
[15] Miller, *Biblical Introduction*, p. 329.
[16] *Ibid.*, pp. 329-330.
[17] *Ibid.*, p. 334.
[18] *Ibid.*, pp. 338-339.
[19] *Ibid.*, p. 344.
[20] Robert Young, *Young's Analytical Concordance to the Bible* (Eerdmans Publishing House, 1955), p. 51.
[21] David Otis Fuller, *Which Bible?* (Grand Rapids: Grand Rapids International Publications, 1970), pp. 40-41.
[22] *Ibid.*, p. 41.
[23] A. O. Schnabel, *Has God Spoken?* (San Diego: Creation-Life Publishers, 1974), p. 38.
[24] S. I. McMillen, *None of These Diseases* (Westwood: Fleming H. Revell, 1963), p. 11.
[25] *Ibid.*, p. 13.
[26] *Ibid.*, p. 15.
[27] *Ibid.*, pp. 17-18.
[28] *Ibid.*, pp. 21-23.
[29] Alfred Martin, *Daniel, the Framework of Prophecy* (Chicago: Moody Press, 1964), pp. 85-86.
[30] Henry Morris, *Biblical Cosmology and Modern Science* (Grand Rapids: 1970), p. 72.

[31] Paul Ehrlich, *The Population Bomb* (New York: Ballantine Books, Inc., 1968), p. 18.
[32] Herman John Otten, *Baal or God* (New Haven, Mo.: Leader Publishing Co., 1965), pp. 216-217.
[33] Frederick Owen, *Abraham to the Middle East Crisis* (Grand Rapids: Eerdmans Publishing Co., 1957), p. 316.
[34] P. B. Fitzwater, *Christian Theology* (Grand Rapids: Eerdmans Publishing Co., 1948), p. 40.
[35] Vernon Grounds, *The Reason for Our Hope* (Chicago: Moody Press, 1945), p. 47.
[36] *Ibid.*, pp. 88-89.
[37] G. M. Day, *The Wonder of the Word* (Chicago: Moody Press, 1957).
[38] *Ibid.*, p. 30.
[39] *Ibid.*, p. 33.
[40] *Ibid.*, p. 34.
[41] W. A. Criswell, *The Bible for Today's World* (Grand Rapids: Zondervan Publishing Co., 1965), p. 25.
[42] James Bales, *Atheism's Faith and Fruits* (Boston: W. A. Wilde Co., 1951), p. 72.
[43] *Ibid.*, p. 76.
[44] *Ibid.*, p. 78.
[45] *Ibid.*, p. 79.
[46] *Ibid.*, pp. 79-80.
[47] *Ibid.*, p. 84.
[48] *Ibid.*, p. 85.
[49] *Ibid.*
[50] *Ibid.*, p. 88.